WADE HAMPTON'S
IRON SCOUTS

WADE HAMPTON'S
IRON SCOUTS

--------------------✦--------------------

CONFEDERATE SPECIAL FORCES

D. MICHAEL THOMAS

THE
History
PRESS

Published by The History Press
Charleston, SC
www.historypress.net

Copyright © 2018 by David Michael Thomas
All rights reserved

Cover images courtesy of the Library of Congress.

First published 2018

Manufactured in the United States

ISBN 9781467139380

Library of Congress Control Number: 2017960105

This book is dedicated to family members of the past and the present. Those from the past served as Confederate soldiers who, by their faithful service, left a legacy of honor and inspiration for future generations.

Private J.M. Thomas—Present at Appomattox
Corporal William V. Cabe—Mortally wounded at Malvern Hill
Lieutenant Colonel David C. Haskins—Captured at Vicksburg
Private R.J.F. Wall—Present at Appomattox
Major J.H. Hannah—Present at Bennett Place
And many worthy others.

The present-day inspiration is my wife, DeeDee, who has been beside me with encouragement, support and thoughtful suggestions from the beginning.

CONTENTS

Introduction   11

1. April 1861–October 1862   15
2. November 1862–January 1863   18
3. February 1863   29
4. March–July 1863   35
5. August–November 1863   43
6. December 1863–January 1864   52
7. February–March 1864   57
8. April–May 1864   63
9. June 1864   70
10. July–August 1864   73
11. September 1864   81
12. October–November 1864   85
13. December 1864   91
14. January–April 1865 (Virginia)   94
15. January–April 1865 (The Carolinas)   98

Epilogue   105
Annotated Roster of Hampton's Scouts   107
Notes   127
Bibliography   137
Index   141
About the Author   144

Mention having been made in my Report of the good conduct of my scouts, it is proper & just that in a narrative of the operations of the cavalry some acknowledgement should be made of the services of these men, who were so zealous, so bold & so intelligent. The mere record of their services would swell this paper to too great a size & to give even their names would occupy too much space, but I desire to declare that they were of incalculable use to me & that they were in general earnest, active & devoted. Living constantly within the lines of the enemy, no movement escaped their observations & I was kept regularly appraised not only of the position, but of the strength, organization, & often even of the very purposes of the enemy. Nor were their operations confined solely to the collection of information for they were constantly engaged in active hostilities & several most brilliant affairs were conducted by them.

—*Lieutenant General Wade Hampton, from the* Connected Narrative of Wade Hampton III, *Hampton Family Papers, South Caroliniana Library, University of South Carolina.*

Introduction

T his work is about a small, platoon-size detachment formed from Wade Hampton's Deep South cavalry officially designated simply as Hampton's Scouts. Their Yankee foe, in grudging admiration, called them Hampton's "Iron" Scouts. With a normal standing complement of about twenty men in the field at any one time, just seventy-two men served in its ranks over the twenty-eight-month existence of this detachment. A study of these men is fully warranted for three very compelling reasons. First, their perspective of the war was unique in that it was mostly from within Union lines. Second, one can arguably state that this was the most dangerous service in the entire army. Finally, when the Scouts spoke, Generals Wade Hampton, J.E.B. Stuart and Robert E. Lee listened attentively.

Hampton's Scouts were an integral part of the Army of Northern Virginia, serving as a major component of the comprehensive intelligence network designed and utilized by Lee, Stuart and Hampton from very late 1862 until the war ended in April 1865. The wide array of responsibilities, roles and missions allow them, with full justification, to be termed Confederate Special Forces. The value and impact of their wartime service far exceeds what their small numbers might imply.

Historians have long known of their existence but little else. No comprehensive books or in-depth magazine articles on their service have been written. They are best known for their role in Hampton's Great Beefsteak Raid of September 1864, in which Sergeant George D. Shadburne, the second commander of Hampton's Scouts, received well-earned recognition. Hampton's biographers and others also noted their actions in the March 1865 Battle of Monroe's Crossroads, but little else of their service is mentioned except in passing references. Why, then, has their full story not been presented until now? The short answer is that there is no clear paper trail. Like any special forces component, their activities, reports and operations were deliberately kept secret. That sort of information was strictly intended for Lee, Stuart and Hampton. Their organization and structure was that of a detachment, not a permanent command. As such, there were no muster reports, periodic reporting requirements or other recordkeeping needs. On the rare occasion a Scout might be in camp, he was prohibited from discussing his activities except with those who had a need to know. Finally, their small numbers contributed to the lack of information on them. Eight of Hampton's Scouts died in service, and of the remainder, probably no more than thirty were still alive in 1900 when it became possible and acceptable for old Confederates to present their wartime experiences to the public. Postwar accounts from only nine former Iron Scouts are known to exist.

The basis for this work is from two books written by former Confederate soldiers. The first, *Autobiography of Arab*, was published in 1901 by E. Prioleau Henderson, who presented his four-year wartime service as seen through the eyes of his horse, Arab. Henderson served as a sergeant in the Hampton Legion Cavalry Battalion and the Second South Carolina Cavalry, spending about fourteen months as a scout for Hampton, and wrote the text entirely from memory. *Arab* is unique in that it provides a glimpse into Iron Scouts' activities from January 1863 through December of that year. The other book, *Butler & His Cavalry in the War of Secession, 1861–1865*, is a collection of postwar newspaper and magazine articles, letters, recollections and other accounts pertaining to the cavalry commands led by Major General Matthew Calbraith Butler. Published in 1909 by U.R. Brooks, a former courier under Butler, it includes many contributions from several of Hampton's Scouts who, in their own words, provide accounts of some of their memorable wartime experiences.

Together, Henderson and Brooks preserved the essentials of Hampton's Scouts, but neither provided a full perspective. The daring and courage necessary to perform some of their deeds is evident within the accounts, but more often than not, the reader cannot place the date, location or background circumstances of the actions described. A close study of the Compiled Service Records for each Scout had positive results. Dates and locations of events such as death, wounds or capture were obtained. These records also provided indisputable confirmation to many of the accounts provided by Henderson and Brooks and offered sufficient encouragement for an in-depth review of the *Official Records*. A detailed search there, surprisingly, found nearly a dozen Scouts mentioned by name. A similar search of the *Richmond Daily Dispatch*, Richmond's largest and most comprehensive wartime newspaper, yielded accounts not found elsewhere and provided corroboration of others. A wide search for accounts from other newspapers, diaries, letters and other sources found only a few, but immensely valuable, references to the Scouts and their service.

Questions remained, however. Just how important were the accomplishments of the Scouts? Surprisingly, biographies of Lee, Stuart and Hampton have little mention of them. However, lengthy and detailed study of the *Official Records* prove these generals considered all their scouts as the eyes and ears of the Army of Northern Virginia, and it is profoundly clear that, for Lee and Stuart, Hampton's Scouts were a major asset.

Taken together, these sources provide a clear view of the Scouts and with a more focused perspective. The accounts given by Henderson and Brooks in their books hold up extremely well to scrutiny, as do accounts from other sources.

This, then, is the first full and in-depth study of Hampton's Scouts. It is not a complete history because those involved took too much to the grave with them. Still, what is available allows a chronological, connected and accurate outline of their invaluable service and operations throughout the various phases of the war.[1] Rich in detail in some areas, there are disappointing gaps in others. Nonetheless, it is hoped this work clears much of the fog shrouding them for so many years while providing long due recognition of brave men.

It is thought another platoon of scouts, those belonging to General Fitzhugh Lee, was formed at the same time and for the same purposes as Hampton's. While Hampton's men were from the Deep South commands (both Carolinas, Georgia, Alabama and Mississippi), Fitz Lee's platoon consisted entirely of Virginians. Unfortunately, records and accounts of their wartime service in sufficient quantity and detail for a unit study have proven to be elusive. It is certain that the two platoons enjoyed a friendly relationship and cooperated extensively with each other. A variety of accounts attesting to the mixing of the platoons on some missions is found, and several of the Virginians are named by Hampton's men in postwar accounts as riding with them. The scant evidence available, however, gives no indication to the operational history of Fitz Lee's detachment.

The *Official Records* contain a wealth of correspondence from J.E.B. Stuart and Robert E. Lee pertaining to scouting reports. Alas, one encounters a frustrating dilemma when reviewing these often incredibly detailed reports because Stuart rarely identifies his sources other than with the terms "my scouts," "scouts" or "a scout." In effect, he considered the platoons of Hampton and Fitz Lee in the same manner as his individual scouts: they were all *his* scouts. Occasionally one can surmise with reasonable certainty which of the detachments gathered information alluded to by Stuart, but the specific men providing it remain unknown. For the sake of clarity, specific references to those Scouts who served as Hampton's special forces are capitalized.

1

April 1861–October 1862

Any study of the cavalry arm of the Confederate Army of Northern Virginia should start with its creator, James Ewell Brown Stuart. When the war began, both the North and South expected it to be decided in a single battle, and priorities went to building the infantry and artillery commands. Cavalry, the most expensive branch of the army to outfit and maintain, was deliberately kept to a minimum. Expectations were that cavalry would serve mainly as escorts, couriers, guides and local scouts. J.E.B. Stuart changed the perception of cavalry quickly for the Confederacy. As colonel of the First Virginia Cavalry, then later as commander of the Cavalry Brigade, he earned accolades from many of his superior officers for his fighting qualities and ability to provide military intelligence. His dash and daring soon made him a darling throughout the South, but to the senior officers in the army, it was his concise and accurate reports on enemy activities, dispositions and other tactical information that made him an invaluable asset. It was understood that his cavalry, in fact, was the eyes and ears of the army.

By October 1862, J.E.B. Stuart enjoyed a well-earned reputation as a hard-riding, hard-fighting leader whose exploits were legendary. What was not publicly realized at the time, and is often overlooked today by many, is that Stuart served in another capacity in the army: he was the de facto chief of intelligence for the Army of Northern Virginia. Robert E. Lee had his own band of individual scouts and spies and was a voracious reader of captured northern newspapers, but in the end, it was Stuart's cavalry that he most

Major General James Ewell Brown Stuart, CSA. *Library of Congress.*

depended on. The fresh, detailed and accurate information in their reports provided Lee with a high-quality overview of his blue-coated foe. Stuart's successes from mid-1861 through the end of the Maryland campaign in 1862 led Lee to place unbridled confidence in the young cavalier, for Stuart not only obtained vital information through his various resources but also accurately interpreted it.

Stuart used two methods of gathering military intelligence. First, he used reconnaissance in force on a regular basis, sending or even leading commands ranging in size from just a few men to one thousand or more. These forays deep into Union territory provided a clear view of enemy dispositions, strengths and activities.

Stuart developed a second source of keeping tabs on his enemy with individual scouts. These were young men possessing the traits and characteristics of Stuart himself. They were energetic, bold and daring, cool in combat, very intelligent and especially efficient in their scouting. Within this loose band were scouting legends Frank Stringfellow, Channing Smith, Redmund Burke and John S. Mosby, all Virginians. Additionally, there was William Farley from South Carolina and John Burke, a Texan. These men, and others, gave Stuart a nearly unimpeded view into Union army movements, unit dispositions and activities. Acting independently, some dressed in captured Yankee uniforms or even in civilian clothes to accomplish their missions. Upon their return, Stuart debriefed them and, with his keen and analytical mind, blended their valuable and timely data with reports received from other sources into a clear, complete and uncluttered image of enemy activities, threats and weaknesses. Summaries of these findings quickly found their way to Robert E. Lee. Together, these two methods allowed Stuart to closely monitor a wide front and, at times, to see far behind enemy lines.

November 1862–January 1863

A study of the circumstances facing Lee and Stuart's cavalry in late 1862 is rather shocking: their cavalry commands were in deplorable condition. On November 10, Robert E. Lee clearly stated the situation and expressed his concerns in two letters. In the first, to Secretary of War George W. Randolph, he wrote, "The diminution of our cavalry causes me the greatest uneasiness. General Stuart reports that about three-fourths of his horses are afflicted with sore tongue, but a more alarming disease has broken out among them, which attacks the foot, causing lameness.… Unless some means can be devised of recruiting [standing down for rebuild and recovery] the cavalry, I fear that by spring it will be inadequate for the service of the army. Horses are so scarce and dear that the dismounted men are unable to purchase them."[2]

In the other, addressed to Major General Gustavus W. Smith, Lee went even further: "The diminution of our cavalry from a disease among the horses is lamentable. I learned…today that the colonel of the Ninth Virginia Cavalry reported only 90 effective men for duty. While the pressure of service is so great upon the cavalry, I see no means of recruiting it."[3]

The hardships of constant operations, poor forage and lack of rest had taken a heavy toll on the horses. Additionally, Stuart's small stable of "individual scouts" was insufficient for the growing needs of the Army of Northern Virginia. While fresh intelligence was of the utmost importance, Stringfellow, Farley and their elite compatriots could not be sent out on a never-ending series of missions. These men, as proven invaluable assets to

General Robert E. Lee, commander of the Confederate Army of Northern Virginia. *Library of Congress*.

the army, had to be carefully husbanded for special purposes. Stuart utilized other troopers from his cavalry, especially from the Fourth and Ninth Virginia Regiments, as temporary scouts in time of need for missions of short duration and limited distance from the front lines.

Lee and Stuart were caught flat-footed when Union general Ambrose Burnside began his move on Fredericksburg on November 15, undetected. Stuart had to scramble every resource he had to get a handle on things and, over a period of several days, recovered nicely. He and Lee saturated Burnside's flanks and rear with scouts cobbled from various sources, including men from the Signal Corps, to observe movements of the massive Union army and monitor supporting Union vessels. Some historians think the scouting detachments from Hampton and Fitz Lee were involved, but no hard evidence of their presence has been found. Through the extraordinary and highly successful efforts orchestrated by Stuart, Lee based his plan of action on solid knowledge and soundly defeated Burnside at the Battle of Fredericksburg. Stuart and Lee had learned a lesson and recognized the need to increase the army's surveillance capabilities to prevent being caught off guard again.

We have no record of conversations, correspondence or deliberations leading to one of the most important and far-reaching decisions of the Lee-Stuart brain trust: maintaining small detachments of scouts behind enemy lines *on a permanent basis* for the purposes of gathering and reporting military intelligence material. While it is not known when or by whom this concept was first proposed, it is certain that the idea was born from sheer necessity.

Examination of available records indicates the starting point for these scouting units was most likely in mid-December 1862, immediately following the Battle of Fredericksburg. No written order for their formation is found, but without doubt Stuart, by now a major general commanding a division, directed his two brigade commanders, Wade Hampton and Fitz Lee, to form detachments of brave men capable of withstanding the rigors of these duties, and each quickly complied.

Few details concerning the formation of Hampton's Scouts are known with certainty, but each is critical to understanding the early Scouts. Hampton knew many of the men in his brigade well, especially those from the original Hampton Legion Cavalry, which had merged with other commands to form the Second South Carolina Cavalry. Further, since taking command of his brigade the previous summer, Hampton utilized local scouting on a regular basis and had a good feel for who best fit the requirements needed for this new role. With his brigade scattered and some of his regiments nearly

Wartime photograph of Lieutenant General Wade Hampton III, CSA. *Library of Congress.*

exhausted, Hampton filled the ranks of his platoon-sized detachment mostly with trusted men from the Second South Carolina Cavalry.

Sergeant William A. "Bill" Mickler (pronounced Mike-ler) of Company B, Second South Carolina Cavalry, was designated as Hampton's chief of scouts. Sergeant E. Prioleau Henderson, of the same command, wrote emphatically that Mickler "commanded the first scouting party Gen. Hampton ever sent out. The Sergeant's first party consisted of only five men."[4] Another important detail is that Mickler and his men received invaluable assistance very early on from a trio of Fitz Lee's scouts. Henderson added, "Bob [Towles], a member of the Prince William Cavalry [Company H], 4th Virginia Regiment, with two others from the same command, Dick and Joe Shephard, all three regular scouts for Gen. Fitz Lee, voluntarily attached themselves to Mickler's little band."[5]

Hampton's selection of Mickler proved to be a superb choice for this type of special duty assignment. After Mickler's enlistment in the Hampton Legion Cavalry as a twenty-one-year-old private in June 1861, his promotions to corporal and sergeant in short order reflect efficiency and leadership ability. His courage and concern for his fellow soldiers are demonstrated by his actions during the Battle of Barbee's Crossroads in November 1862, in which his regiment, engaged in close combat, was forced to beat a hasty retreat when Union reinforcements unexpectedly arrived. Prioleau Henderson vividly described what happened next:

> *While crossing a low muddy piece of ground, Private Eldred Simkins' (of our company) horse was shot dead under him. The enemy was in close pursuit of us, and Simkins, unable to extricate himself from the dead horse, was about to be captured, when Sergt. W.A. Mickler dashed back to his rescue, and springing from his horse, extricated Simkins from his, then taking him up behind him on his grey, brought him safely off the field in the very face of the Federals.*[6]

No mention of the detachment's first mission assignment or its date is found, but indications suggest that Hampton and Mickler started on a small-scale basis to determine the viability and operational needs of such an assignment prior to committing a larger force. The Scouts certainly needed a base of operations central to their assigned territory, roughly triangle-shaped, extending southwesterly from Alexandria to Fredericksburg and Rappahannock Station. With the Potomac River forming the eastern border and the Orange & Alexander Railroad marking the western, the area of coverage encompassed about 1,100 square miles. These boundaries covered major portions of Prince William, Fauquier and Stafford Counties and some of Fairfax. Brentsville, in Prince William County and about five miles southeast of Manassas Junction, seemed to fit the need perfectly. It put the Scouts in position to monitor the railroad, a stretch of about

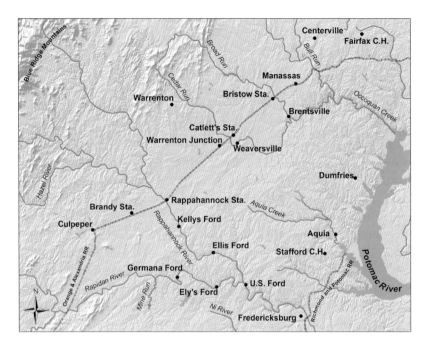

Operational area of Hampton's Scouts, December 1862–June 1864. *Courtesy of Scott Williams and the Chesterfield Historical Society of Virginia.*

fifty miles between Alexandria to Warrenton Junction with several stations along the way. Furthermore, Brentsville was close to major Union base camps at Occoquan and Dumfries. Two other sites of importance, Aquia Landing and the general area of Stafford County Court House, were about 25 miles away.

Mickler's initial tasks were to find a staging area around Brentsville and friendly Virginia civilians who could be counted on to provide food and shelter, as well as forage for their horses, when needed. The assistance and guidance from the Virginia Scouts, Towles and the Shephard brothers, were invaluable. Native sons of this area, their intimate knowledge of the citizenry and terrain ensured a short transition period for Hampton's men. Also of benefit was that the region was one in which the Hampton Legion Cavalry had previously spent substantial time, acquiring both a good reputation and many friends in their own right. Finally, Mickler and his men took note of which civilians to avoid because of their Unionist leanings. Rolling hills, fertile fields and productive farms accented this area of operations, but there were also dense forests, numerous streams and wide-open spaces. A profound knowledge of the terrain and its population was critical to operate safely.

Just exactly what, though, were Stuart's expectations of Hampton's Scouts once they were positioned and organized? Certainly, the primary mission was to gather and report information on the enemy, particularly regarding troop dispositions, concentrations, sudden changes or movements. Also included was identification of potential targets of opportunity for Confederate cavalry raids and, doubtless, warning of any immediate or pending threat to the Confederate army. This sort of work is by necessity carried out by stealth, as substantial effort is required to avoid detection while observing an enemy. Their early actions, though, clearly indicate Stuart added a secondary mission of conducting, as he often phrased it, *la petite guerre* (the small war), a term meaning unconventional or guerrilla warfare. This task vastly increased the perils and difficulties of an already challenging endeavor.

Wade Hampton was fully aware of the difficulties this multipurpose assignment presented to his Scouts, but had full confidence in Bill Mickler to make Hampton's Scouts a success. Mickler seems to have accomplished his primary needs in the Brentsville area without delays or problems. He and his small party apparently established firm ties with friendly civilians, familiarized themselves with the lay of the land and reported to Hampton that the preliminary work was completed. Analysis of the various accounts clearly indicates that at this point, almost certainly still in December, Hampton increased his scouting detachment from squad size to a platoon. It is clear Mickler was allowed substantial input in the selection of those who would serve with him. Hampton and his regimental commanders appointed fourteen Scouts in addition to Mickler from the Second South Carolina, with all but one having ties with the old Hampton Legion Cavalry. They were Sergeants Thomas L. Butler, E. Prioleau Henderson, J. Dickerson Hogan, J. Marion Shirer and J. Calhoun Sparks; Corporals Josiah Beck and Huger Mickler (Bill's brother); and Privates George M. Crafton, James R. Dulin, A. Bernard Henagan, R. Cecil Johnson, Simeon E. Miller, J.S. Shoolbred and John C. Willingham. Privates George J. Hanley, William P. Parks and James M. Sloan were appointed from the First North Carolina Cavalry, while Private Wallace Miller was assigned from the First South Carolina Cavalry.[7]

This was a formidable force. Each man was a seasoned veteran who had demonstrated his courage on the field of battle. One source familiar with Hampton's Scouts wrote, "When a man got such an appointment…it simply meant he was cool and courageous at all times. No ordinary man could fill the position."[8] All were well mounted and armed with two or more Colt .44-caliber revolvers.[9] Some carried a shoulder weapon, usually a double-barreled shotgun, but sabers were left behind.

The first mention of Hampton's Scouts can be pinpointed to the morning of January 9, 1863. Although a minor skirmish, multiple accounts of this action can be found, indicating it nonetheless was considered especially notable. Early that day, a patrol from the First Michigan Cavalry consisting of six men led by a lieutenant entered Brentsville with the express intent of eradicating Mickler, who was known to be in the area with a few Scouts. The patrol's timing was poor, as two Scouts happened to be in Brentsville when they arrived and, unobserved, rode to alert Mickler. Upon hearing of the enemy presence, Mickler, with five men, rode straight to Brentsville with intentions of meeting the Yankees' challenge. Mickler approached Brentsville using the tree line as cover and spied the Yankees in a relaxed state, with all but one dismounted and the officer sitting while reading a newspaper in front of the hotel. The Scouts were within one hundred yards of the hotel before being spotted, and at that point, they charged. In the ensuing mêlée, Mickler, Sergeant Calhoun Sparks and Private Jack Shoolbred, well ahead of the other Scouts, killed three Yankees and captured two, both of whom were wounded. A long chase ended with the taking of the officer, but one man escaped.[10] Mickler's little party, with its prisoners, did not linger at the scene of action and shortly afterward turned the prisoners over to part of Hampton's main force cavalry in the area. Unfortunately, the prisoners were lost during a chance encounter with a large Union cavalry force that afternoon.[11] This shootout, the first documented record of Hampton's Scouts, clearly shows they were already known and identified by the Yankees. How, and for how long, are questions remaining unanswered.

The three principals in this daring action, Mickler, Sparks and Shoolbred, were honored in several ways for their daring success. Their regimental commander, Colonel Matthew C. Butler, issued a General Order recognizing these men for their courage, coolness and gallantry. Further, he issued a glowing report of the affair to his brigade commander, Wade Hampton, who passed it to J.E.B. Stuart. Ultimately, it wound up with General Robert E. Lee, who replied with a gracious letter of acknowledgement and appreciation for the "gallant conduct" of these men.[12]

The Scouts certainly were aware of massive Union presence when they began operations but likely didn't know quite how badly the odds were stacked against them. Union general W.W. Averill reported on January 10, 1863, "I have 600 men on picket duty and 500 scouting."[13] Encounters

Catlett's Station, an area Hampton's Scouts monitored and passed through many times. *Library of Congress.*

with Union forces over the next couple of months were common, of short but intense duration, and usually initiated by the Scouts, who utilized the element of surprise to the fullest. The presence of the Scouts added an additional menace to harried Union commanders already facing continual threats from guerrillas and small raids from frontline Confederate cavalry commands such as the famous Black Horse Troop (Company H, Fourth Virginia Cavalry from Fauquier County). There is no doubt the Scouts were recognized by the Yankees as a capable, daring and ever-present foe.

Bill Mickler put his organizational skills to use early on to meet the many challenges of leadership in a situation fraught with danger. Not all the men on the Hampton Scouts roster were available to him on a daily basis. Several were termed "occasional scouts," meaning they rode with their parent

and captured Pope's baggage, A.R. Waud

commands until, and unless, called for by Mickler.[14] Usually working with about fourteen men in the field, he sent small teams of Scouts in different directions on daily reconnaissance missions. These teams consisted of two to four men, with the number involved dependent on the mission parameters. At least in the early stages of their clandestine work, none wore Union uniforms. Mickler personally led two special types of missions: running missions and fighting missions. He was heard to say when preparing for an extended mission one day, "Mind, I am going on a running, not a fighting trip this afternoon, and you well know what an open county it is. I only want a few men on fast horses."[15] This indicated a patrol seeking particular intelligence, and contact with the enemy was to be avoided if possible. A fighting mission, however, was one targeting a specific enemy unit or position, with Mickler carrying as many men as could be assembled.

Each Scout was responsible for his own meals and the care of his horse. The various accounts document they often slept in fields, barns and forests.

At times, during inclement weather or when Union patrols were not around, they slept at the homes of friendly civilians. Before settling in for the evening, they made sure Mickler knew where they were in case of an urgent need or sudden danger. The men never stayed in the same place two nights in a row and generally avoided anyone with Unionist leanings. Obtaining sustenance proved to be no problem, as they often enjoyed fine meals at the dining table of their civilian friends or had it provided where they intended to sleep if away from the house. There were also the saddlebags of Yankee prisoners, which often were full of delicacies beyond bacon and hardtack. Forage for the horses was easily obtainable, and blacksmithing needs could be resolved without tremendous effort.

Mickler set up other policies and procedures affecting the Iron Scouts organization. His chain of command was a short one. He reported directly to, and received orders from, only General Hampton, who, in turn, relayed the reports to Stuart. Mickler's commands to his men were perceived as being issued by Hampton's full authority and obeyed without dissent. Additionally, Mickler made his elder brother, Huger, responsible for getting prisoners to Confederate lines and devised methods of rotating his men back to their regimental camps for short periods. Men assisting Huger Mickler in moving prisoners to friendly lines could take a day or two to catch up on rest. Mickler rotated men at regular intervals to carry reports to Hampton, who allowed them to rest their horses and themselves before sending them back with messages. Mickler usually kept a couple of men close by in case he needed to redirect the efforts of a team on distant patrol, send an urgent message to Hampton or issue a general recall to multiple teams in preparation for a fighting mission. One other policy believed to have been established in these early days was that the Scouts ride in no less than pairs.

Most of Mickler's policies became standard practice for Hampton's Scouts through the rest of the war. His relationship with his men was a good one, and the sparse accounts testify to the bond of complete trust forged between them. Mickler led from the front and cared for his men, both necessary elements of successful leadership. The Scouts' small numbers masked their strength, which was based on efficiency. Scouting teams, regardless of size, knew exactly what their missions entailed and the roles each man would play before they mounted up. Mickler could transform his platoon from several data-gathering teams spread over many square miles into a potent strike force within just a few short hours. Anything they did was deliberate and calculated, for there was simply no room for impulsive or careless action in an already dangerous environment.

February 1863

Hampton's Scouts quickly settled into a productive pattern of carrying out their assigned missions. Their covert operations required stealth, silence and avoidance of contact with their blue-coated foe. Enemy camps were closely watched for any change in normal activities, such as cooking extra rations, distribution of ammunition or any other undertaking associated with major operations. Southbound trains were monitored for supplies, reinforcements, artillery or horses. Northbound trains received the same attention to detail, thus allowing Stuart to maintain a regularly updated status on the enemy strength, disposition and, above all, intentions. Stuart was anxious to ensure that the Yankees never again stole a march on him.

Union lines were porous, and despite numerous forward picket posts and heavy patrols to their rear, Confederate scouts easily navigated their way through and behind Union lines in early 1863. Upon entering an area, Sergeant Mickler and his men searched for and noted the reserve picket positions. Large picket posts presented problems and were avoided, but the smaller reserve picket positions, usually manned by four to six men, were considered vulnerable and targeted for capture on the return trip. The sudden disappearance of pickets in supposedly safe areas was maddening to the Federal commanders and filled their men with tension and apprehension. These continued losses adversely affected morale of the Union cavalry and caused friction among some of the commanders. Prisoners were a source of information, often yielding valuable intelligence, and the Confederate

Aquia Creek Landing, a major Union supply and logistics facility closely monitored by Hampton's Scouts. *Library of Congress.*

cavalry gladly accepted the captured horses, weapons and accouterments. These forays became not only standard operating procedure for the Scouts but also regularly assigned missions lasting to war's end.

Hampton's Scouts gained confidence in themselves and quickly became aware of the immense opportunities to hurt their enemy. Taking care to avoid the numerous large Union scouting parties in their area, they showed determination and energy in carrying out their duties. J.E.B. Stuart orchestrated some of their missions in conjunction with scouting missions of Fitz Lee's scouts. Other endeavors, though, were at the discretion of Sergeant Mickler.

Union patrols usually traveled in large numbers, primarily because the Scouts regularly ambushed their smaller ones. The *Official Records* carry numerous reports in this time frame from Union commanders leading from 50 to 150 men in their search for Hampton's men. Mickler's band soon learned the Yankees, despite their numbers, were reluctant to pursue them through dense woods. Therefore, they avoided open fields and roads when possible, preferring to travel through the forested areas. Numerous engagements between the Scouts and their foe took place. Several chance encounters resulted in the Scouts turning their horses and riding to outrun their pursuers. If that failed, they headed into the nearest forest.

One example of their aggressiveness involved three Scouts intent on carrying the war to their enemy despite terribly cold weather. Sergeant Tom Butler, with Privates Cecil Johnson and Wallace Miller, attacked a Union scouting party from the First Michigan Cavalry near Bacon Race Church, capturing two and running the others back to their main camp. While Butler carried the prisoners to Confederate lines, Johnson and Miller planned to capture a four-man picket they had spotted earlier. However, that idea was shelved when they found the picket had received about thirty more men in the interval.

Backing away, they spent the night in the woods, hoping to ambush another small patrol in the morning, but those hopes were dashed by the arrival of a sizeable scouting party, also from the First Michigan, entering the wood line apparently searching for them. Johnson and Miller hunkered down as the blue-coated riders spread out in search of their trail. One of those riders came across the Scouts, but before he could sound an alarm, both Johnson and Miller placed a revolver in his face, ordered him to dismount and demanded silence. The rider complied and was taken with his horse behind some thick bushes, where the entire party successfully hid until the Yankees gave up their search and moved on, never realizing they were short a man.[16]

Small Union cavalry patrols were such easy prey for Hampton's Scouts that Union commanders mandated a fifty-man minimum patrol strength. *Library of Congress.*

Early February was a busy time for Mickler and his men. On February 7, Hampton wrote to Stuart, "My scouts have captured 25 prisoners in the last few days and killed 6 of the enemy."[17] Immediately afterward, they successfully ambushed sizeable Union cavalry forces on three occasions. In one instance, Mickler, with ten men, caught a sixty-four-man company by surprise and totally routed it.[18] In another, Mickler, this time with fifteen men, detected a large Union force described as a regiment approaching a ford near Greenwood and quickly placed his men for an ambush. One of the Scout participants vividly recounted the action:

> *Mickler concealed his men in the thick pines on the bank of the run, and waited until they rode in and halted to water their horses, when he ordered his men to fire. Imagine the scene that ensued. Mickler's intention was to fire on them, and then "get away." But seeing such a stampede among them, he ordered a charge, and we ran them into their picket lines near Dumfries. Oh! what a glorious race it was. We found the killed and wounded of the enemy all along our route, as we returned from the pursuit with our prisoners. It was a 4 or 5-mile race.[19]*

The Scouts continually penetrated Union lines and roamed freely in their quest for information needed by Stuart and General Robert E. Lee. At the same time, they became a force to be reckoned with in combat, and their reputation grew not only in Confederate estimation but in the eyes and minds of their enemy as well.

The Scouts pulled off another stunning ambush on February 13, 1863. This time, the target was a large Union force in the Brentsville area dispatched for the sole purpose of destroying the Scouts. The Federals told civilians their intentions were to "'eat up without salt' Wade Hampton's little band of scouts."[20] Word of the enemy presence and their mission soon reached Mickler, and he issued an urgent recall of available Scouts to meet the threat.

While still gathering his men, Mickler noticed a ten-man squad of Yankee cavalry on the other side of Deep Run, and the Scouts set out for a nearby ford to engage the Yanks. The crossing was difficult, and only three Scouts (Hogan, Hanley and Henderson) were with Mickler when they emerged from the woods to find the enemy in formation with carbines raised and ready to receive them. Nevertheless, Mickler and his small band charged. The Yankees fired, but every shot missed. The Scouts shot three from their horses, and the others turned to flee. Two more blue coats were shot and the remainder captured in the ensuing chase.[21]

The prisoners freely gave away information vital to Mickler before being sent away under guard. They had been placed at the ford to guard against ambushes against the main force when it returned. Several companies of cavalry were patrolling and would eventually return via this route. Mickler, down to fourteen men because of the prisoners, laid out plans for an ambush. Placing eleven men along wooded high ground by the cut, he told them to let the advance guard pass by and to open fire when the main force was in their front. Three others remained mounted with instructions to chase any escaping enemy.

After a wait of a little more than an hour, a Union company came in sight and approached the ambush site unaware of the danger. Prioleau Henderson, dismounted for the engagement, wrote about what happened when the main column entered the ambush zone:

> As ordered, the signal shot rang out, and shot after shot in rapid succession followed, dealing death and destruction to the terrified enemy, from a foe they could not see….Men and horses down; those behind running or riding over those in their front; some trying to ride their horses up the steep slippery bank and never succeeding, but falling back on those below.[22]

The three mounted Scouts gave chase to those escaping this chaotic scene and were soon followed by other Scouts in a pursuit extending to the enemy's heavy picket lines. Returning to the ambush site, Mickler's men recovered weapons and all sorts of accouterments discarded by the fleeing blue coats during the chase.[23]

Hampton's Scouts, in the two actions that day, caused a loss to the enemy of thirty or more men and at least fifteen horses while taking an abundance of valuable accouterments and weapons. In addition to the ten-man squad taken initially, the First Michigan Cavalry reported a loss of seventeen men, one officer and twelve horses from a forty-six-man company. General Robert E. Lee acknowledged this action in his General Order No. 29 on February 28: "A detachment of 17 men…under the brave Sergeant Michael [sic], attacked and routed a body of 45 Federals near Wolf Run Shoals, killing and wounding several, and bringing off 15 prisoners."[24] A Richmond newspaper reported on February 18, 1863, five days after the action, that "twenty-four Abolition prisoners of war arrived at Libby prison yesterday. These followers of Old Abe were captured… after a brisk skirmish by Lieut. Shiver and Serg't Mickler of Col. [Matthew C.] Butler's cavalry."[25]

The Scouts suffered just one casualty that day, the first in their short existence. Regimental Color Sergeant Calhoun Sparks, Second South Carolina Cavalry, received a wound to the chest during the chase yet captured a Yankee in the oddest circumstances. Shortly after being wounded, Sparks lost consciousness and fell from his horse. Soon after, he happened to wake up just as a Yankee rode out of the woods and was passing him. Sparks, with his pistol still in his hand, rose on an elbow and demanded the rider's surrender. The surprised man complied with the demand and sat silently on his horse in front of the bleeding and prostrate Sparks for about thirty minutes until other Scouts arrived. One Scout wrote, "Well, if you ever saw a mad man, it was that Yankee dragoon when he found out that pistol pointed at him was empty."[26] Mickler obtained medical assistance for Sparks and placed him in a safe house for several weeks until he could travel to Confederate lines for further recuperation. Sparks was unavailable for field duty again until December.[27]

Another incident from around this time tells more of the special pluck possessed by the Scouts. Lieutenant Bob Shiver led Private Hugh Scott (an occasional Scout), Sergeant Woody Barnwell and Private Gillespie Thornwell on a particular mission requiring them to travel on foot. Crossing the Rapidan River on a raft of logs they put together, they soon completed their assignment. On the return to friendly lines, a reserve picket of four men was taken along with their horses and equipment. Now mounted, the little party with their prisoners began the trek back to safety. However, when they reached the river, they found themselves in a dilemma because a large Union picket had been placed unexpectedly at their planned crossing spot. After some thought, Shiver turned the prisoners loose and led his party of Scouts at a gallop—to the astonishment of the Yankee manning the position—completely through the group from its rear to the river. Upon reaching the ford, the Scouts shot the vidette and completed the crossing without any casualties.[28] Undoubtedly, this little affair caused some frayed nerves and loss of sleep for the Union troopers manning the picket post.

In their first two full months in the field, Hampton's Scouts were wildly successful. Taking prisoners, carrying out ambushes, gathering military intelligence and supplying the Confederate cavalry with horses and equipment came naturally to the men. The dangers of their missions were understood and accepted without complaint. However, they could not have foreseen the changes and challenges just around the corner.

4

MARCH–JULY 1863

On January 26, 1863, Major General Joseph Hooker received command of the Union Army of the Potomac. He immediately went to work to restore morale, entice deserters to return and reinvigorate an army badly mishandled by his predecessor, Major General Ambrose Burnside. His efforts, some of which were not so subtle, substantially reorganized the army in a relatively short period. Additionally, Hooker mandated that the lax security along his outer lines be replaced by much more aggressive measures and increased vigilance, with senior officers being held accountable for results. The emphasis of these edicts fell mostly on his strengthened cavalry.

Redoubts at key positions, manned with artillery and infantry, were built. Additional outposts and picket positions were established, while infantry positions were moved forward. Surprise raids were made on farms of Southern sympathizers in hopes of capturing some of Hampton's Scouts, with dire threats to the lives and property of those suspected of harboring Confederate soldiers. The Scouts countered this measure by staying with Union sympathizers. One Union cavalry regiment, the Eighth Illinois, gained much notoriety over the next few months for its callous treatment of civilians. This regiment was especially active in the fight against Hampton's Scouts and other Confederate forces in the general area.

Very little is found on the specific activities of the Scouts in the months of March and April. The *Official Records* contain numerous reports from Lee and Stuart regarding Hooker's army, and much of the detail within

Typical wartime redoubt. General Joseph Hooker utilized positions like this to prevent Confederate scouts from entering his lines in 1863. *Library of Congress.*

them could only have come from Mickler and his men. Enemy patrols, consisting of large numbers and quite wary of their surroundings, became near impossible to ambush. Prioleau Henderson explained the situation concisely: "The enemy down in our scouting grounds had ceased coming out in small detachments, that we could attack—for you know we could not *always pitch into a regiment.* They even had the Orange and Alexandria Railroad guarded, as well as a constant patrol of horsemen to keep us out of their lines."[29]

Several other things came about in this period, though. Bill Mickler was declared an outlaw, and a reward was placed on his head.[30] Secondly, the Yankees began calling Mickler and his men Hampton's "Iron Scouts." The precise origin and date of this moniker has never been found, but the reasoning could only be because the Scouts seemed impervious to Union bullets. This name was never used by the Scouts themselves, but they certainly took no offense to it.

Sergeants Prioleau Henderson and Bill Mickler were nearly captured in separate incidents while staying at friendly houses when Union cavalry showed up without warning. However, both men avoided detection by hiding in the bedding of the hosts while the premises were searched.[31]

Sensing a buildup within Union positions, Hampton strengthened his scout detachment and sent a squad to Stafford County to monitor enemy activities. Sergeant Woody Barnwell, with eight others, went there but could stay only a short while before being forced to withdraw, after which they joined Mickler's platoon.[32]

March 30 was a stressful day for Mickler and his men. They had just returned from a patrol lasting several days and were resting when word of an approaching Union regiment was received. Riders were dispatched to provide warnings and a rendezvous recall to the Scouts staying at various homes across the county. Mickler, accompanied by Prioleau Henderson, reached several Scouts in time, but upon reaching the farm where Corporal Josiah Beck and Private Jack Shoolbred were staying, they saw a sizeable Federal contingent surrounding the house and outbuildings. Mickler tried to distract the Yankees by firing at them from long range but to no avail. Henderson described the ensuing action:

> Directly we saw a squad of Yankees leave the dwelling and make for the stable…some distance off. Just as they got near the stable, we saw Beck ride out on a fine mare he had recently captured from our friends, the 1st Michigan cavalry. Of course, the Yankees halted in surprise; and, to our surprise, we saw Beck dash towards them and through them, passing in his flight through other squads, and in close pistol range of those at the dwelling house.…Though hundreds of shots were fired after him, [Beck] escaped. The enemy then returned to the stable…and [came] out with Shoolbred and his horse, as prisoners.[33]

Beck's unlikely escape through a hail of bullets certainly added to the lore and reputation of the Iron Scouts. Henderson's account adds that some of Fitz Lee's scouts were also captured that day, and Mickler, with several others, set up an ambush intending to free those captured. However, the Yanks did not pass by until after dark, and the ambush was called off for fear of hitting the prisoners.[34]

March was indeed a bad month for the Scouts, as Hampton lost several other men to capture. Sergeant Willie Haskell and Privates Jim Dulin and Jim Guffin were taken separately over a two-week period.[35] Fortunately for them, their stay as Union prisoners of war was short, and they were exchanged in a matter of weeks.

One substantial recorded successful encounter in this month concerned Woody Barnwell's squad while in Stafford County. Barnwell, along with five other Scouts (Sergeant Willie Haskell and Privates Gillespie Thornwell, Newton Fowles, John Bradley and Roswell Logan), had just finished breakfast at a rural farm and were preparing to depart on a patrol. While standing on the front stoop and giving thanks to their hosts, a large number of Yankee cavalry rode up with guns drawn, calling for the Scouts to surrender. Barnwell and his men responded by drawing their own revolvers, shooting about a half-dozen riders from their horses and charging. At that point, the rest of the Yankee force fled. Though the stoop was pockmarked with bullet holes from Yankee guns, neither the Scouts nor the host family were hit. This was another classic example of the Iron Scouts' legacy.[36]

Hampton's Scouts were not the only ones having difficulty in entering and remaining in enemy lines. Fitzhugh Lee's scouts reported the same problem. Robert E. Lee and Stuart became quite concerned and called on their other assets to find out what was going on with Hooker's massive army. Robert E. Lee's March 29 letter to Secretary of War James Seddon contained a bombshell. Lee wrote, "The scouts report that it is very difficult to get within the enemy's lines, as their pickets are posted within 50 steps of each other. These circumstances may account for my getting no information."[37] On April 2, in a letter to President Jefferson Davis, Lee wrote, "Their lines are so closely guarded that it is difficult to penetrate them. Their pickets are within sight of each other, with dismounted men in the intervals."[38] Fitz Lee, with much of his brigade, tried to force his way into the enemy lines to gather badly needed intelligence but was forced to retire well before fully accomplishing his mission.[39]

The entire month of April was a nightmare for Lee and Stuart, for they received precious little military intelligence on Hooker's army. It seemed an impenetrable wall of blue-coated soldiers blocked all avenues of access to its interior. Information received, in bits and pieces, indicated a major thrust involving cavalry and infantry. Despite calling on every source available, Lee and Stuart were mainly in the dark as to Hooker's intentions. Making things worse was that Hampton's cavalry brigade was in a stand down to the rear because of the deplorable condition of its horses and Longstreet's Corps was absent on detached duty near Suffolk. Further complicating the situation were swollen rivers and streams fed by incessant rains, which brought the activities of each army to a near standstill. In essence, Lee and Stuart were operating nearly in the blind and felt terribly vulnerable in the weeks leading up to the Battle of Chancellorsville.

In late April, Hampton's Scouts received their most unusual order of the war. Word was sent to them to rendezvous with Major John Mosby, the famed Gray Ghost, who was such a thorn in the side of the Yankees, in an area termed "Mosby's Confederacy." Mosby's Rangers, formed just four months earlier, had quickly established a reputation for their daring while earning the confidence of Lee and Stuart. On April 26, Stuart directed Mosby to hit the enemy near Warrenton Junction. In his orders to Mosby, Stuart further stated, "Information of the movements of large bodies is of the greatest importance to us just now."[40]

The purpose of the proposed attack was to create concern and confusion within Hooker's rear. Mosby had only a small force, which Stuart reinforced with Hampton's Scouts and other smaller commands. Mosby later wrote he mustered seventy or eighty on the day of the attack.[41] One of his lieutenants, James Williamson, later figured a total of ninety-eight men were in Mosby's party.[42]

Mosby launched his attack on the morning of May 3 while the Battle of Chancellorsville was in full fury and not far away. The attack was successful beyond all hopes and, after hard fighting, received the surrender of almost three hundred men of the First Virginia Cavalry (U.S.). While in the act of securing them, however, the Confederates were surprised when two fresh Union regiments suddenly appeared. Abandoning their prisoners, Mosby and those with him took to their horses, fleeing in a manner that was basically every man for himself. Mosby lost about twenty men from his command in the counterattack.[43]

Hampton's Scouts also suffered casualties that day. Private Lamar Stark was captured. Privates Simeon Miller and Gillespie Thornwell were both wounded and captured. Thornwell's wound, to his stomach, was serious. Miller recovered from his wounds quickly and was soon exchanged. Poor Thornwell, son of a prominent South Carolina pastor, lingered in an Alexandria hospital only a short while before expiring, thus becoming the very first of Hampton's Scouts to be killed in action. Found in his Compiled Service Records is a notation stating that his "body [was] taken away by friends."[44]

Upon learning of Thornwell's death, Wade Hampton sent a three-page letter of condolence to his parents on May 19, outlining the circumstances of their son being wounded and captured. Included was a newspaper clipping from a Washington area newspaper attesting to young Thornwell's death.[45] After the war, the family returned his remains to South Carolina.

The Scouts needed several days to regroup after the fight at Warrenton Junction and took a well-deserved stand-down period.[46] The annals relating to their service are mostly blank from then until late July. What is known is that some of the Scouts were recalled to their regiments in the following weeks. Some of the captured were exchanged in May or June and eventually returned to the Scouts. Still, Hampton and Mickler needed to reconstitute the detachment. The accounts indicate that three men were appointed to fill the permanent Scout vacancies left by Calhoun Sparks, Simeon Miller and Gillespie Thornwell. One was Private Franklin "Gus" Black of the Jeff Davis Legion Cavalry. The others were Sergeant Dick Hogan and Private Newt Fowles of the Second South Carolina Cavalry.[47] Each had been part-time Scouts and proven fit for the role. One other vacancy in the detachment occurred in the spring. The date is unknown, but Corporal Huger Mickler, elder brother of the Hampton Scouts' commander, was killed in a nighttime ambush by Federal troops while patrolling with two other Scouts, who were driven from the scene. When Bill Mickler and other Scouts were able to come to the ambush site, they learned the beloved corporal had been buried in a nearby church cemetery by local citizens. Prioleau Henderson noted that the uniform Huger Mickler was wearing when killed was a gift that his Virginia sweetheart had recently made for him.[48]

In early June, the Scouts carried out an action resulting in the capture of a large Yankee squad. Bill Mickler, Jim Sloan, Prioleau Henderson and others were in the detail bringing the prisoners to Confederate lines and, after delivery of the prisoners, took time to visit their various regiments. Unexpectedly, they quickly found themselves amid two notable events. They watched the June 8 Grand Review of the Cavalry, a spectacular event showcasing the majority of Stuart's cavalry. However, the next day they were in close combat with the enemy during the totally unexpected and furious Battle of Brandy Station. Sloan was captured in the fighting that day, bringing the number of losses through death, wounds or capture in the Scouts to ten in barely a month.[49]

Shortly afterward, with the commencement of the Gettysburg Campaign, the Scouts were completely recalled and returned to their regiments.[50] In the ensuing weeks, two Scouts, both from the Second South Carolina

Private Cecil Johnson. Killed in action at Upperville, Virginia, in June 1863. *Library of Congress.*

Cavalry, were killed in action. Private Cecil Johnson died in the June 21 battle at Upperville, and Sergeant Tom Butler was killed in the cavalry clash on July 3 at Gettysburg. Johnson was buried by local civilians at a house near where he fell. His father, chaplain of the First South Carolina Cavalry, expressed satisfaction with the burial site, and presumably, young Johnson is still there.[51] Butler was buried on the field at Gettysburg, but his body was retrieved at war's end and returned to his family.[52] Additionally, Dick Hogan suffered several broken ribs at Gettysburg and was unavailable for service for an extended period.[53]

The Gettysburg Campaign closed the first chapter of Hampton's Scouts. Their performance throughout their seven-month existence was remarkable in every way. Bill Mickler's quiet, steady and confident leadership proved his mettle not only as gallant soldier but as a quality leader.

There was another casualty at Gettysburg, one that brought despair and concern to the Scouts. General Wade Hampton received several serious wounds that kept him away from field duty until November.

AUGUST–NOVEMBER 1863

Hampton's Scouts were reactivated soon after the return of Lee's army to Virginia and positioned for duties in Fauquier and Stafford Counties. There are gaps pertaining to their activities over the next several months, but enough documentation is available to confirm their operations were no less vigorous than those of the first part of the year. Gathering military intelligence, conducting guerrilla warfare and bringing in prisoners along with their horses, weapons and accouterments remained the core elements of their duties. General J.E.B. Stuart is believed to have added another mission in this period, signifying implicit faith in Hampton's Scouts, by tasking them with safe delivery of dispatches between the Confederate high command and certain individuals well behind Union lines. One notable appointment to the Scouts was Private William A. Bolick of the First South Carolina Cavalry, who, within a short while, showed his own style of daring and intrepid pluck.[54]

One other change in this period, instituted by Abraham Lincoln on July 30, 1863, was the dissolution of the Dix-Hill Cartel. This certainly caused concern to the Scouts because of the dangers they faced each mission. The cartel was the program set up to arrange exchange and parole of prisoners of war between the two nations. A man captured by either side usually found himself released under parole within a few weeks. Now, with this practice stopped, anyone unfortunate enough to be captured was likely to be held indefinitely. In fact, some Confederates taken at, or just prior to, Gettysburg languished as prisoners of war for two full years. General prisoner-of-war

Aikens Landing on the James River, a prisoner-of-war exchange site. Most Scouts captured and exchanged arrived here on vessels like this. *Library of Congress.*

exchanges were resumed only in February 1865 after thousands of prisoners from both sides perished of disease and other causes in the interval.

The first mention of the Scouts after Gettysburg is found in a report dated July 27, 1863, by a Union colonel. In it, he acknowledged a five-man Union patrol was ambushed and attributed the attack to a squad of four South Carolinians seen in the area earlier that day. The ambush resulted in at least two men captured. An interesting point in this report is that it identifies the ambush site as near the house of Richard Colvin, a prominent citizen near Cedar Run.[55] Colvin's youngest son, John, would soon be one of Hampton's Scouts.

A report from General J.E.B. Stuart, dated September 5, relates another Scout action in late August. In it, Stuart wrote, "About 10 days ago a party of scouts from Hampton's brigade under Hogan [Sergeant Dick Hogan], captured the entire mail of Kilpatrick's [Union brigadier general Judson Kilpatrick] division en route from Catlett's Station to Hartwood Church, showing that this division was encamped near Hartwood, and other valuable information, which has been forwarded to the commanding general."[56] Stuart's report reveals two important facts. One is that Dick Hogan was well known to Stuart and (presumably) Robert E. Lee as an effective scout. Secondly, it shows Hogan in the position of authority thus indicating earned trust from Mickler and Hampton.

After returning from Gettysburg, the entire Army of Northern Virginia shared the personal grief and concern of their beloved general, Robert E. Lee, whose son, Brigadier General William Henry Fitzhugh "Rooney" Lee was being held as a hostage by the U.S. government. Rooney, recuperating from a wound received at Brandy Station, was taken prisoner on June 26 by a Union cavalry raid designed for the express purpose of making the capture. His younger brother Robert E. Lee Jr. barely escaped being taken at the same time. At this point, Rooney became a pawn in one of the ugliest episodes of the war.

Two Confederate officers taken prisoner in Tennessee shortly before Rooney Lee was captured were charged as spies, subject to hanging. Following denial of an appeal to Lincoln's government for the lives of the two men to be spared, the Confederate government threatened to execute two Union prisoners if the execution of the officers was carried through. The United States' response was a statement that Rooney Lee would be executed if the South carried through its threat. Revulsion and anger stemming from this callous threat spread across the entire South, which was powerless. In the end, the Confederate officers were executed and the Confederacy took no retaliatory measures.

Stuart's cavalry felt tremendous anguish over the situation with Rooney Lee. He was "one of them" as well as the son of their army commander. Based on specific and detailed intelligence received from some of his scouts, Stuart devised a bold plan in early September to capture a Yankee general, to be used in securing Rooney's release. Stuart personally formed "a party of 12 select men…under [Captain] Frank Stringfellow" to raid the camp of Union general Joseph J. Bartlett, an infantry commander, for the purpose of making him a prisoner and exchanging him for Rooney Lee.[57] Stringfellow, perhaps the most well known of Stuart's individual scouts, was a perfect

Postwar photo of Major General W.H.F. "Rooney" Lee, CSA, middle son of General Robert E. Lee. *Library of Congress.*

choice for this daring mission. The raiders infiltrated Union lines and, about one o'clock in the morning, reached the Union camp. What then transpired is found in Stuart's post-action report: "[T]he general [Bartlett]...saved himself by precipitate flight in his nether garments."[58] Making no attempt to take prisoners, Stringfellow did take Bartlett's headquarters flag before the raiders departed, shooting in all directions, leaving mass confusion within the camp. Stuart added, "Not a man of the select 12 was touched."[59]

Newspaper accounts claimed at least twenty Yankees were shot in this foray.[60] Besides Stringfellow, only one other man from this "select group" is identified. He was Private William A. Bolick, First South Carolina Cavalry, a man who had been in Hampton's Scouts just a few short weeks but, in that short time, earned a reputation noticeable by Stuart.[61] Rooney Lee was finally exchanged in February 1864.

The Scouts continued to harass targets of opportunity and picket posts during this time, with a great deal of success. Sergeant Dick Hogan found a secluded, abandoned two-story house in Stafford County to temporarily house prisoners and named it Libby Prison No. 2. Holding captured soldiers there allowed the scouts to wait until twenty-five to thirty prisoners were in hand before taking them to Confederate lines. Eventually, the Yankees learned of the house and ended its use.[62]

October was a month marked by a couple of events that served as omens for things to come. The war, now in its third year, was becoming more brutal. The string of campaigns, occasional raids and never-ending patrolling and picketing over the past year had especially hardened the cavalry commands of each side. Regiments swore revenge and no mercy for members of certain opposing regiments if captured. Southern men, especially the Virginia

Wartime sketch of a small Union picket post. Such positions were favorite targets of Hampton's Scouts. *Library of Congress*.

cavalry, were well aware of the trepidations, threats and brutality toward Southern families wherever Union forces went.

One October night, Sergeant Dick Hogan, accompanied by Privates Hugh Scott, George Hanley and Wallace Miller, were scouting deep in Union territory. They crossed the Rappahannock on foot and passed the pickets along the riverbank but didn't have to go much farther before capturing a captain, a sergeant and two privates along with their horses. Leaving Scott, at this time an occasional Scout, to guard the prisoners, the others departed to continue their mission. Their time was productive, for the trio returned with three more horses, and the entire party left the area before daybreak.

Scott and Hanley were detached to carry the prisoners in while Hogan and Miller did some more patrolling. Still deep in Union territory, Scott and Hanley stopped twice during the day for meals for themselves and their prisoners at the homes of local citizens. However, Hanley simply disappeared along the way and Scott had sole responsibility of controlling the prisoners while watching for threats and being unable to relax even a moment for several hours. The young Scout successfully reached Confederate lines with his prisoners only to find Fitz Lee's cavalry where Hampton had been when the mission started. He learned that the two commands had been shifted and Hampton was now fifteen miles away. Upon informing the prisoners they would be turned over to the Virginians, the captain was openly shaken and begged Scott not to do so. Giving his oath that neither he nor his men would attempt to escape if Scott would take them to Hampton's cavalry, the captain pleaded passionately for Scott to reconsider. It soon became apparent to Scott there was justification to the captain's fears because of bad blood between the captain's command and the Virginians. The fate of their lives was squarely in his hands.

Ultimately, Scott took them to Hampton's location the next morning and let his prisoners eat breakfast at his company's camp before turning them over to the provost marshal. Scott recorded their parting:

> Captain Mason said to me, "This business you are in will cause you to either be killed or captured." He gave me the address of his wife and said, "If you are ever captured, write to her and you will not suffer for anything….If I am ever exchanged and you are captured, hunt me up, and I will let you walk through the camp and turn you [loose]. I have been treated far better than I ever expected to be treated by a Johnny Reb."[63]

Another scouting mission from this period was of such significance that it quickly became widely known at the headquarters of both Robert E. Lee and Union general George Meade. Lee noted it with pleasure, but for Meade and his subordinates, it left a bitter taste.

In late October, one of Hampton's Scouts, Private William Bolick (one of Stuart's select men who attempted to capture a Yankee general the previous month) and Isaac Curtis, one of Fitz Lee's scouts from the Ninth Virginia Cavalry, were together on a mission near Weaverville close to Meade's headquarters. On their own initiative, they decided to enter and scrutinize Meade's camp. About sunrise on October 31, the pair, wearing Union overcoats and unchallenged, passed the double row of pickets guarding the camp perimeter. Bolick wrote they were "whistling so as not to cause suspicion."[64] After satisfying their curiosity and not wanting to press their luck too long, they began their exit, not realizing they had come within a few hundred yards of Meade's personal headquarters. However, three tents behind a house caught their attention, and they made a spur-of-the-moment decision to leave their mark by capturing those sleeping in the tents.

Riding to them, Bolick and Curtis dismounted and roused the sleeping Yankees with an order to quietly dress and saddle their horses, for they were "needed for a special purpose."[65] The unsuspecting bluecoats, cattle guards for a nearby herd, did as they were told and rode right out past the picket lines with Bolick and Curtis only to learn shortly afterward that they were prisoners. One man later escaped, but the remaining five Yankees were safely delivered to Confederate lines—complete with their fully equipped horses and weapons.

Bolick wrote a short report regarding this foray, and J.E.B. Stuart endorsed "this act of gallantry, which is only one of many which are almost daily performed by our daring scouts."[66] Bolick's report also stated that he and Curtis considered capturing the cattle herd but felt that was too much for two men with prisoners to handle. This is the first known instance of the Scouts disguising themselves as Union soldiers. General Robert E. Lee sent Bolick's report to the War Department with a stamp of approval, but his counterpart, General George Meade, had to endure the embarrassment of reading about the affair in Northern newspapers.[67]

The roster for Hampton's Scouts had changes in this period. Jim Sloan was captured in August for a second time but escaped Point Lookout less than a month later. James Dulin was captured a second time in September and spent several months as a prisoner until buying his way to freedom. Several others were recalled to their regiments. Filling vacancies that fall

Old Capitol Prison in Washington, D.C. Many captured Scouts were held there before being exchanged or sent to prisoner-of-war camps. *Library of Congress.*

were Sergeant James Brent and Private Rufus B. Merchant of Cobb's Legion cavalry and Sergeant John Pierce and Private W.W. Russell of the First South Carolina Cavalry.[68]

A shroud of fog covers the personal activities of Sergeant Bill Mickler from Gettysburg through November. He is not mentioned in any account written by a Scout in this time nor is there a mention of the Scouts being recalled for a "fighting mission." However, in October Mickler received promotion to second lieutenant under the provisions of the Valor and Skill Act of 1862. This promotion was different than most because it was not a result of election by his compatriots but recognition by the Confederate government for his demonstrated valor and leadership skills. He was one of ninety enlisted men from the entire Confederate army who received this type of promotion to officer status in 1863. This well-deserved selection was based on his aggressive and successful encounters with the enemy in January.[69] The promotion, however, put his scouting status in jeopardy. Removal from this critical position at such a pressing time would have been a calamity for the Scouts, and fortunately, Mickler remained in his position for the time being.

The month of November was especially hectic for the Iron Scouts, as it found them in a highly fluid situation as the opposing armies maneuvered to gain a decisive advantage over each other in what is called the Mine Run Campaign. Moves and countermoves, punctuated with several severe clashes, resulted in a stalemate by the first part of December, at which time the armies went into winter quarters. Hampton's Scouts, however, continued their work despite the inactivity of the main armies.

One event of note was that Wade Hampton, recently promoted to major general, returned from his medical furlough in November. However, neither he, Bill Mickler nor anyone else could have guessed that the next couple of months would usher in a series of drastic changes for the Scouts.

DECEMBER 1863–JANUARY 1864

Major General J.E.B. Stuart's report on the Mine Run Campaign mentions a dispatch received from "a very reliable scout [Mickler]" on the night of December 1 warning of the possibility of a Union attack.[70] Though the attack did not take place, this is a telling remark for it indicates two major points. First, it confirms that Mickler's name and reputation were well known to both Stuart and Robert E. Lee. Second, by emphasizing the source of the dispatch, Stuart was able to justify subsequent actions on his part. This is one of the rare instances in which Stuart actually named his Scout source. From this point, Mickler's records become somewhat confusing. Henderson wrote in *Autobiography of Arab* that Mickler was wounded while trying to capture a pair of Yankees inside a house, and Sergeant Calhoun Sparks, just recovered from his wound the previous February, was killed in the same engagement. Unfortunately, Henderson provides no date of this affair, and Mickler's service record gives conflicting dates of this action. It might have occurred on January 6, 1864, but the more probable date is December 16, 1863.[71] Sergeant Mickler was replaced as commander of Hampton's Scouts on Christmas Eve 1863 after a year of superb and effective leadership, and any reason for this change other than because of the severity of his wound would seem to be unfounded conjecture. The wound, a gunshot to the leg, was severe enough to keep him from field duty for over six months.

Major General Wade Hampton, now a division commander, selected Sergeant George D. Shadburne of the Jeff Davis Legion as his new chief of scouts. The reasoning behind this selection remains a mystery. Shadburne, a native Texan, enlisted in the Jeff Davis Legion Cavalry on December 19, 1861, at the age of twenty-one and, over time, rose to the rank of sergeant. No record or indication of any sort is found that he ever served as a Scout under Bill Mickler. Though his service record has nothing indicating he stood out in any way, his regimental commander, Lieutenant Colonel J. Frederick Waring, undoubtedly provided a ringing endorsement of Shadburne's qualities to Hampton. In quick fashion, Shadburne would display his own style of personal courage, battlefield savvy and audacity.

Hampton faced difficult circumstances at this time, and these likely played a big part in Shadburne's selection. One would have expected him to name one of the several capable and experienced Scouts in the platoon, but Hampton had several complicating factors to consider. In addition to losing Mickler and Sparks, Hampton lost other experienced Scouts just a few days apart. Private T.S. Cloyd (Jeff Davis Legion) was captured on December 13, and J. Newton Fowles (Second South Carolina Cavalry) was taken the next day.[72] With these losses in such a short span, there is little doubt that Hampton realized his scout detachment would require a substantial overhaul. Further, with manpower in his two South Carolina regiments nearly depleted, he was probably worried that they might soon have to recall their men from scouting. Adding considerably to his quandary was that he was actively trying to send the First and Second South Carolina Cavalry regiments back to the Palmetto State for complete stand down and rebuilding while bringing three full regiments in South Carolina to Virginia to replace them. This move, if approved, would take the twelve South Carolinians from the Iron Scouts in one fell swoop, leaving the platoon in a precarious and unacceptable position. It makes sense, then, to say that Shadburne's appointment was substantially based on the future as anticipated by Hampton, and a fresh influx of proven men from other than his South Carolina regiments was needed to keep his Scouts at effective strength.

No record is known of the conversations between Hampton and Shadburne regarding Shadburne's appointment. Hampton would certainly have provided him his standing orders and certain guidance while satisfying himself that Shadburne understood what was expected of him and his men. Part of that conversation probably was a request by Shadburne to have Private Thomas Thistle from Shadburne's company in the Jeff Davis Legion, presumably a trusted friend, detached as a scout along with him. The two men were officially appointed together on December 24, 1863, just eight days after Bill Mickler was wounded.[73] Thistle's appointment gave Shadburne the luxury of having at least one close confidante from the Jeff Davis Legion.

The records are hazy, but the roster of Hampton's Scouts at the time of Shadburne's appointment probably consisted of the following sixteen men: Sergeant John H. Pierce and Privates William Bolick, Joseph A. Twiggs and W.W. Russell from the First South Carolina; Sergeants J. Dickerson Hogan and E. Prioleau Henderson and Privates John A. Bradley, J.S. Shoolbred, Hugh H. Scott, J.T. Gufffin, A. Bernard "Barney" Henagan and John C. Willingham of the Second South Carolina; Sergeant James H. Brent and Private Rufus B. Merchant of Cobb's Legion; and Privates William P. Parks and James M. Sloan of the First North Carolina. These men were all seasoned Scouts and veterans of many successful missions. Shadburne's transition as their commander was made easier by their knowledge, experience and cooperation. He also inherited a working system established, molded and refined by his predecessor with results that satisfied Hampton, Stuart and Robert E. Lee. Still, Shadburne faced the daunting task of adapting his personal talents and skills to meet the challenges he would soon be facing.

December 1863 was an active month for Hampton's Scouts in a wide range of other activities. They returned to Prince William County, an area with many friends and fond memories. Several clashes with their blue-coated foe after returning are recorded by Prioleau Henderson. In one, five Scouts (Henderson, Hogan, Shoolbred, Henagan and one other not named) were on patrol when they came upon a widow and daughter whose farm had just been raided by a squad of enemy cavalry. The culprits had rummaged through the house and barn, carrying off everything they could, including sheets, clothing, poultry, bacon, flour and other items. Upon learning the Yanks had departed just a few minutes earlier, the Scouts spurred their horses to a shortcut and caught up with them. In the ensuing chase, five of the enemy were shot, another was captured and most of the stolen goods were recovered.[74]

In another instance, Henderson and Scout Joe Beck, along with Private William Thorne of the Fourth Virginia Cavalry and one of Fitz Lee's Scouts, attempted to capture a Union colonel and his orderly who strayed away from their main force close to Mount Holly Church near Kelley's Ford. The effort failed, and in the resulting shootout, the colonel was killed, but Henderson captured his horse, a fine, well-saddled roan. Henderson rode that horse for several weeks before word reached him that the dead colonel's regiment had promised to execute any Confederate caught riding it. Henderson promptly sold the horse, and it eventually wound up in South Carolina.[75]

Henderson wrote fondly of "a jolly good time"[76] during Christmas and New Year's celebrations, as there was "plenty to eat and drink."[77] The local citizens opened their homes to the Scouts, providing food and merriment to the weary soldiers, who had to dodge Yankee patrols and picket posts to reach some of those homes. The holidays went by quickly, and the new year began quietly.

The month of December brought another responsibility to the Scouts. Their new task was to guide dismounted cavalrymen into enemy territory for the express purpose of securing horses from the enemy.[78] This practice allowed dismounted men to be remounted and then take prisoners and captured equipment back to Confederate lines, thus freeing the Scouts to proceed to their other assignments within the enemy lines. While quite dangerous, this method proved effective and became invaluable in keeping Hampton's division mounted and armed.

January 1864 was a month of transition for Hampton's Scouts, and eight names, all from the Jeff Davis Legion, were added to the roster. They were Sergeants S.L. Carroll, J.J. Harrison and Daniel F. Latham and Privates John L. Chapman, John S. Elliott, A. Champion Knapp and Archibald Waller. Another man, William H. Hodges, joined as well, but he was reduced in ranks from first sergeant to private for accepting the appointment.[79] The Iron Scouts were now at their largest strength since being formed. Everyone expected the armies to begin maneuvering again in the spring, and such strength would be a necessary asset.

Highly capable and well-loved Private A. Bernard "Barney" Henagan left the Scouts, probably in early January 1864, after being promoted to captain, with authorization to raise an independent squad of scouts. This remarkable opportunity is one that could not possibly have taken place without the full backing of J.E.B. Stuart. Henagan apparently filled his squad and became well known to Union forces until being captured on March 20. His jailers at Old Capitol Prison in Washington received a memo about him from the Washington District provost marshal: "You will receive and confine…the person of Captain Andrew Barnabas Hannigan [sic], Second South Carolina Cav, noted Guerilla Chief, Terror to the neighborhood in which he was taken. Boasted that he could not be captured alive. A dangerous man and will escape if he has the opportunity."[80] Henagan was later transferred to Point Lookout, where he was held until June 1865.[81]

One other note of interest from this time is that it appears Scout J. Dickerson "Dick" Hogan became Shadburne's second in command. There is no documentation attesting to it, but from this point on, Hogan is found having authority not granted to others. Later accounts show Hogan as having Shadburne's full and complete trust.

7

February–March 1864

Two more men from the Jeff Davis Legion, Privates William H. Hord and A.J. McCoy, were detached to Hampton's Scouts in February and quickly learned that, despite a cold, bitter winter, the Scouts remained busy with myriad missions.[82] Most of their efforts were centered on the core of their general responsibilities and usual missions, in which they showed they were no less alert and aggressive than before. Several noteworthy engagements with the enemy are found in the records, and each is a powerful story conveying a clear picture of just how energetic, daring and enterprising Shadburne and his men were.

The first is related by Scout W.W. Russell in a 1916 newspaper article. The gist of the article is that in February 1864, Dick Hogan located a Union cavalry command camped in a vulnerable location with lax security. Russell wrote that Hogan, with about forty men, passed through about three hundred yards of brush and past the outer sentries to the camp late at night. After charging and briefly engaging the enemy, Hogan called for, and received, surrender of nearly the entire camp. Most of the surprised and shocked Yanks stacked arms in surrender, but one company to the rear rallied and charged. In the fresh mêlée, Hogan suffered a bullet wound to his chest and lung. The Scouts were soon forced to withdraw, and Russell, now in command, carried Hogan away from the scene to their horses. Russell remembered that "three or four of us got Hogan into a saddle and I rode behind him."[83] They rode several hours to the house of a friendly civilian but had to move away the next day when Union patrols came searching for them. Using fence posts to fashion a litter, Hogan was carried to a decrepit, secluded and abandoned house nearby. Ultimately, he spent two months well behind Union lines unable to be moved but was nursed and cared for by Russell and another friend before being moved to the residence of a friendly civilian for another month. Wade Hampton sent a surgeon to examine and treat Hogan while promising that he would use his entire force if needed to get Hogan back to friendly lines. Hogan eventually recovered sufficiently and returned to duty a couple of months later.[84]

Former Iron Scout commander Bill Mickler would have applauded the brazen nighttime attack. In addition to suffering numerous casualties, the enemy force was likely embarrassed and demoralized. Russell's claim that there were about forty men in the attacking party may be true, but certainly not all of them were Scouts. There are later instances of Scouts asking for a squad, platoon or even a company of regular cavalry to assist them in hitting large Union forces, and this might be the first occasion of such cooperation.

Several other elements stand out in this action. One is that this attack was led by Sergeant Hogan, a clear indicator of his high status in the eyes of Shadburne and Hampton. The size of Hogan's force and the nature of the attack denote a great deal of preparation and planning, likely requiring personal authorization or involvement from Wade Hampton. Finally, the attack gave notice to the Federal commands that Hampton's Scouts were as dangerous as ever, even with a new commander.

Another February encounter took place on the fourteenth, just outside Brentsville. Shadburne led about ten men on a nighttime trek to a site offering a fine ambush location. Just three Scouts were mounted, but the plan was to mount the others with horses captured in the ambush of a sizeable Union patrol in Brentsville. Shadburne sent his mounted men (Privates Hugh Scott, William Bolick and another unidentified rider) to draw them out. The first attempt, early in the morning, failed to get a response. A second attempt, several hours later, was successful. The Yankees gave chase and rode straight into the trap. The Scouts wreaked havoc on the blue-coated foe in a perfectly timed ambush, and the mêlée was over quickly. Scott, in a postwar account of this action, claimed seventeen of the twenty-one Yankees were killed. A Union report about this engagement admits to two men killed and four others wounded. Despite the successful ambush, the Scouts took just one horse and Bolick was killed. Lacking sufficient horses and knowing additional Yankees would soon show up, the Scouts left Bolick's body, carefully wrapped in a blanket, deep in the woods and departed the area.[85]

What happened next reflects the closeness within Hampton's Scouts and clearly indicates the respect Bolick had from his peers. Two days after the ambush, the Scouts returned with a coffin in a two-horse wagon and recovered Bolick's body. They drove him to his Virginia sweetheart's home at Arrington's Crossroads and buried him there. This trip of about ten miles was made in broad daylight despite being well behind enemy lines and in an area known to have frequent enemy patrols. The Scouts, known to avoid unnecessary risks, obviously felt that providing a suitable burial for one of their own outweighed the dangers.[86]

Just two weeks later, Hugh Scott found himself involved in one of the most infamous episodes of the war. The Union high command authorized a cavalry raid on Richmond in which it was hoped that about 13,000 Union prisoners of war would be freed from Libby Prison and Belle Isle. Additional goals were to kill President Jefferson Davis and his cabinet and to destroy Richmond by fire. This raid, known as the Dahlgren-Kilpatrick raid, called for a feint toward Charlottesville by substantial Union infantry and cavalry forces. The plan was intended to lead Stuart's cavalry away from the area, thereby opening the way to Richmond for the two prongs of the raid. Colonel Ulrich Dahlgren led about 500 men in one prong, and Brigadier General Judson Kilpatrick had 3,500 men in the other. Stuart, with only a small part of his cavalry available because his Virginia regiments were on a winter furlough, took the bait, leaving Richmond nearly completely uncovered on February 28.

Scott and Private Dan Tanner, an occasional Scout from Cobb's Legion, were on a mission that day on foot, and shortly after crossing the Rappahannock River on logs after dark, they encountered Kilpatrick's large cavalry column. Realizing something was afoot but not knowing what led them to discuss whether they should continue with their assigned mission or divert their attention to this powerful concentration. After deciding to forego their original assignment, they relieved a couple of Yankee horsemen at the rear of the lengthy column of their mounts and joined it. Riding long enough to determine that a major threat was indeed in the making, the pair broke away and rode hard to Hampton's headquarters, where they informed him of what they had seen.[87]

Reports from other Scouts reached Hampton shortly afterward with enough amplifying information to confirm the severity of the threat. Hampton tried, without success, to reach Stuart with a series of telegrams explaining the situation, and Stuart continued his chase, oblivious to the disaster threatening Richmond.[88] About 10:30 p.m. on February 29,

Hampton, without orders and entirely of his own volition, could stand it no more and initiated a chase despite the cold, rain, sleet and snow. With 306 cavalrymen from the First and Second North Carolina Regiments, a section of Hart's Battery and Privates Scott and Tanner, Hampton had barely 10 percent of Kilpatrick's force. Two questions certainly must have been in his mind: Can I catch Kilpatrick before he does great damage? Secondly, what will I do if I catch him?

Late on March 2, Kilpatrick dismounted his weary troopers near Atlee's Station, about seven miles above Richmond, allowing them to build fires, cook, pitch tents and sleep. Hampton, by pushing his little command, made up for lost time. He linked up with Colonel Bradley Johnson's sixty horsemen from the First Maryland Cavalry and found Kilpatrick's camp after dark that night. The little Confederate force approached cautiously, and when a Union vidette was sighted, Hampton called for Scott and Tanner. Scott wrote that Hampton told them, "I want their vidette captured, and I don't want a shot fired."[89] The pair succeeded with their usual proficiency and returned soon afterward with the vidette as a prisoner. Hampton then brought Hart's guns up and, at 1:00 a.m., with his entire force in position, the order was given to fire. Kilpatrick's command, caught completely off guard, put up little resistance and fled into the night. Kilpatrick admitted to losing about four hundred men. Hampton claimed his forces took over three hundred prisoners and many valuable horses, in addition to supplies and weapons. This engagement, coming at the end of a desperate pursuit in the foulest of weather, dashed the hopes of the inglorious Yankee plans and ranks as one of Hampton's greatest achievements. Scott and Tanner certainly made significant contributions toward this success.[90] Other Confederate forces killed Dahlgren and destroyed his command, thus ending the threat to Richmond.

While Hampton's pursuit of Kilpatrick's cavalry was going on, other actions involving his Scouts were occurring. On March 1, five of his Scouts were captured, three in one incident and two more in another. In the first, Sergeants James Brent (Cobb's Legion), S.L. Carroll (Jeff Davis Legion) and John H. Pierce (First South Carolina) left camp on foot in Fauquier County, intending to pass around known enemy pickets, eat supper with a friendly civilian family nearby and, after dark, capture a particular reserve picket before returning with their prisoners and captured horses.

Unfortunately, before getting far, they were sighted by a Union cavalry patrol, which gave chase. The Scouts fled to a wooded area, and as the patrol approached, they exchanged fire at close range. Two of the Scouts used double-barreled shotguns and hoped that would encourage the patrol to abandon the chase. Unfortunately, it was not meant to be. The Yankees spread out on the flanks and began a systematic approach and search that ultimately forced the Scouts from the woods into an open field. Carroll was taken first, and shortly afterward, Brent and Pierce were discovered. Pierce's postwar account of this action describes what happened next:

> *As we rose up out of the straw and briers we were met with a volley of hisses and curses. We drew our pistols, cocked them and were about to fire into the Yankees when* [their captain] *rode up and ordered his men to attention. They paid little or no attention to his orders at first and he even struck several over their heads with the side of his saber before he could command attention. They were the most violent set of Yankees I ever saw, and we were expecting to be shot every minute, yet we intended to sell our lives dearly.*[91]

Ultimately, when Pierce and Brent realized they were not going to be shot, they surrendered and, with Carroll, were held as prisoners of war for the rest of the war.[92]

The other Scouts captured that day were Sergeant J.J. Harrison and Private John A. McCoy, both from the Jeff Davis Legion, who were on a mission near Fairfax. Held at Old Capitol Prison in Washington, Harrison escaped at 3:00 a.m. on August 10, 1864. McCoy was later transferred to Fort Delaware, where he was confined until June 1865.[93]

The bad news kept coming to Shadburne and Hampton. On March 31, they lost yet another Scout to the enemy. Sergeant Daniel F. Latham of the Jeff Davis Legion was captured near Falmouth and held at Fort Delaware until June 1865. Further, A.C. Knapp was recalled to his regiment and assigned duty with the Quartermaster Corps.[94]

Having six Scouts captured and another transferred in such a short period was a terrible blow. However, the worst loss of all was when Shadburne lost all his South Carolinians in one fell swoop that month. On March 17, the Confederate War Department authorized the First and Second South Carolina Cavalry regiments to be returned to their native state in exchange for a new brigade of three fresh and fully manned regiments (Fourth, Fifth and Sixth South Carolina) under the command of newly promoted Brigadier General Matthew C. Butler. Shortly after the announcement, the Scouts from the First and Second South Carolina were recalled to their regiments and began making ready to leave Virginia. Prioleau Henderson wrote that when he returned to his regiment, "The 2nd South Carolina Cavalry… was a mere squadron—the companies barely a 'corporal's guard.'"[95] His company, originally mustering eighty-six men, now carried just fourteen on its roll and only eight were present.[96]

On March 2, Hampton left Virginia to help organize Butler's new brigade in South Carolina, leaving Brigadier General P.M.B. Young as acting division commander. Shortly afterward, General Ulysses S. Grant was appointed lieutenant general and given command of all the Union armies. Grant made his headquarters with the Army of the Potomac under General George Meade and began preparations for a spring offensive, while Robert E. Lee and Stuart paid close attention to reports from all their scouts.

APRIL–MAY 1864

Sergeant George Shadburne was probably ecstatic to have March finally roll over into April, for it was a terrible month for the Scouts. Reeling from the massive losses to his platoon, he was faced with rebuilding Hampton's Scouts, knowing the opposing armies would soon leave winter quarters and campaigning would begin anew. On April 1, his detachment is thought to have consisted of just twelve men. Besides Shadburne, there were Privates John L. Chapman, John S. Elliott, William H. Hodges, William H. Hord, Thomas T. Thistle, Richard S. Torry and Archibald R. Waller, all from the Jeff Davis Legion. Completing the roster were Privates Julius Shakespeare Harris, William B. Parks and James M. Sloan of the First North Carolina and Private Rufus B. Merchant of Cobb's Legion. This roster was the smallest since shortly after the formation of Hampton's Scouts in December 1862. However, there was no letup in Stuart's expectations of them despite the misfortune of losing so many experienced men so quickly. Certainly, all involved had the same question: What can be done to rectify this situation?

The task of providing a full, capable and efficient scouting platoon fell squarely on the shoulders of Major General Wade Hampton, and he responded handsomely. The fact that the platoon was not totally wiped out in March was due to the foresight he demonstrated the previous December. On April 14, 1864, Hampton wrote a lengthy letter to Adjutant and Inspector General Samuel B. Cooper. One item touched on revealed how Hampton planned to strengthen his scouting detachment. He wanted men from the

First and Second South Carolina Regiments, especially his old Scouts, to return to Virginia and continue their service as Scouts and guides for the new brigade. He wrote:

> As General Butler will have a brigade of new troops, I have requested the colonels of the First and Second South Carolina to let me have ten men from each regiment as scouts and guides. These men know the country, and they will be great use to me….I do not care to have them mounted, as they can soon mount themselves in the lines of the enemy….The service of my old scouts is very important to me.[97]

Hampton did not get the twenty men he sought, but he did secure the commitment of thirteen men to leave the comparative quiet of South Carolina for the primary battleground state of Virginia. Among this group were eight experienced Scouts, for whom Shadburne was likely most grateful.[98] They were Sergeant Dick Hogan and Privates James Dulin, James Guffin, T. Bernard King, W. Wallace Miller, W. Walker Russell, Jack Shoolbred and Hugh H. Scott. Though their original scouting service began under Sergeant Bill Mickler, each had served under Shadburne, and their willingness to return must be seen as an endorsement of his leadership.

Three others were solid soldiers and probably had ridden as occasional Scouts before. They were Sergeant James D. McCalla and Privates W. Adolphus Kennedy and William B. Morrow. McCalla, by returning to Virginia, was reduced in ranks to private by his command.[99]

Two other men filling the ranks were Privates Lemuel L. Guffin and L. Pemberton Guffin, who accompanied their brother James. Nothing can be found indicating either previously served in the cavalry or in Virginia, but Hampton apparently accepted them gladly. Known as Jim, Lem and Pem, the three brothers received much teasing from their compatriots.[100]

Two of the thirteen had personal reasons for leaving South Carolina and returning to war-torn Virginia. Bernard King's prewar home was Washington, D.C. A promising young lawyer there, his support of the South led him to leave and join the Second South Carolina Cavalry in Virginia. The other man was James Dulin, a native Virginian whose home was in Fauquier County. Dulin was likely anxious to return, and the opportunity to do so was a relief. Five of his brothers had died in Confederate service. The youngest of these, Billy Dulin, was in the first few days of his Confederate service when murdered by Union cavalry in early 1863 during a skirmish in

Wartime photo of Private Jack Shoolbred, Second South Carolina Cavalry, an original Scout who served faithfully until war's end. *Courtesy of the South Carolina Confederate Relic Room and Military Museum, Columbia, South Carolina.*

the streets of Warrenton. According to witnesses, Billy was shot by a Union officer, Captain (later Brigadier General) Elon Farnsworth, while pinned under his fallen horse and completely helpless. Upon hearing of his brother's manner of death, James swore never to give or request quarter and promised to take the lives of one hundred Yankee soldiers. Those close to him later confirmed he surpassed that number. One source asserted, "The Yanks that he shot seldom needed the services of a surgeon…[and] his deeds of bravery were so dashing and reckless as to often merit the praise of his chiefs, the great cavalry leaders, Hampton and Butler."[101]

There are no known reasons for any others in this group to return to Virginia. The Scouts received no extra pay or other privileges. Their role kept them in constant danger behind enemy lines for weeks at a time. Further, once detached from their commands, they were not eligible for promotion. The South Carolinians could have remained home close to family and sweethearts, enjoyed regular home-cooked meals and slept safely at night far away from imminent danger. Yet they willingly gave all this up to return to scouting in Virginia. It is apparent they believed in the cause for which they fought and felt their contributions as Scouts could make a difference in the war. Whatever their reasons, they were certainly welcomed back by Shadburne and Hampton upon their return in May.

With the Iron Scouts' roster drastically reduced at such a critical time and Hampton in South Carolina, Shadburne was under a huge amount of pressure. He certainly had adapted well to his role, but the demands on him and his small platoon were heavy. He and his men were stretched thin across a large area and faced multiple dangers every single day. No one was aware that some of Hampton's old Scouts would be returning soon, and with full justification, Shadburne and his men probably suffered some anxiety. One source acknowledged, "Too much cannot be said on behalf of our scouts. Nearly every day while on duty a good scout carried information in one hand and his life in the other."[102] However, the Scouts could do only so much with their limited numbers, thereby leaving the Army of Northern Virginia at risk. Shadburne, always a man of action, took an unusual step to remedy the situation.

On April 10, Shadburne wrote a letter to Secretary of War James Sedden requesting authorization to "organize a company to operate in the enemy's lines as scouts for the division"[103] as an independent command. His brigade commander, General J.B. Gordon, enthusiastically endorsed the letter as "most earnestly recommended. Shadburne is a Scout of well-known gallantry and ability, and has had long experience in such duty and is well worthy of promotion."[104] General P.M.B. Young, acting division commander, also added a glowing endorsement of Shadburne's request and concluded, "Sergeant Shadburne has always been a zealous, faithful and gallant soldier."[105] General J.E.B. Stuart, though concurring with the praise of Shadburne, declined to support his proposal. Robert E. Lee also withheld support, and ultimately, the request was denied.[106] By the time Shadburne learned of its denial, the thirteen brave South Carolinians returning to Virginia were nearly ready to resume scouting duties, thus removing the bulk of his concerns. The rock-solid opinion of Shadburne by his generals clearly shows the esteem in which he was held.

Despite their circumstances, Shadburne and his small band suffered no let down in their activities. An April 13 report from a Union captain confirms their presence and his frustration in chasing them. Reporting on the status of his most recent patrol in the Falmouth/Fredericksburg area, it reads in part:

[There is] *but a small force of the enemy on this side of the river. Hunting principally in couples, sometimes in gangs of six or a dozen, skulking about*

*the pines in the day, sometimes at the houses of citizens at night, and never
at the same place two nights in succession….We have hunted these fellows
on horseback and on foot, in highways and byways, by day and night…
and our conclusion is that all the bushwhackers and scouts on this side of
the river are not worth the powder and shot that it takes to blow them up.*[107]

Hampton returned on May 2 and found indications from many different
scouting reports that Meade's army, in its winter quarters around Culpepper,
was preparing an offensive. The various reports found in the *Official Records*
do not identify the originators, but some are almost certainly from Hampton's
Scouts. The *Daily Dispatch* seems to have enjoyed close access to the
Confederate high command; in early May, it ran several articles pertaining to
reports from Confederate scouts in areas specifically assigned to Hampton's
Scouts. On May 4, the newspaper printed the following: "Scouts report that
the enemy have struck their tents in Culpepper, and that the Yankee army is
moving."[108] Meade's army began its movement southward and was quickly
detected. Shadburne sent in a report the next day not found in the newspapers
but recorded in the diary of Colonel Fred Waring of the Jeff Davis Legion:
"Everything has moved to the front. Negros and Indians are guarding the
railroad. Our scouts are in Culpepper Court House."[109] On May 6, the
Daily Dispatch wrote more of the developing situation: "Our scouts went
into Culpepper C.H. [Court House] this morning, capturing about a dozen
stragglers. The scouts report the country about Culpepper C.H. is covered
with debris of the enemy's camps, including clothing and blankets."[110] The
May 9 issue had an article with further details: "Scouts say that the enemy
have abandoned the line of the Orange railway, and no cars are running on
it. It is supposed that Grant now intends to make Fredericksburg his base."[111]
The May 16 issue confirmed that "Grant shows no sign of falling back. Scouts
report him to be receiving no reinforcements."[112] Clearly, Shadburne and his
men were performing in a highly credible manner during this critical period.

Not only were the Scouts effectively patrolling, monitoring and reporting,
they were hurting the enemy in other ways as well. Colonel Waring's wartime
diary has several interesting entries pertaining to Shadburne and his Scouts.
The May 19 entry exulted, "Shadburne has again pitched into the Yanks. He
[his scouting party] killed nine, captured two and got 13 horses."[113] The next
day, in referring to his previous entry, Waring wrote, "Saw Sgt Shadburne &
prisoners. He killed eleven. They were Dutch."[114]

The first great battle in 1864 was fought at the Wilderness on May 5–7
and was quickly followed by another major engagement at Spotsylvania

Major General J.E.B. Stuart's burial site. Image taken shortly after the fall of Richmond. *Library of Congress.*

that commenced on May 8 and lasted until May 21. In an effort to break Confederate communications and threaten Richmond, Union cavalry under General Philip Sheridan moved out, undetected initially, toward Richmond, penetrating to Yellow Tavern just six miles from the city. There, on May 11, Sheridan was intercepted by Stuart with a much smaller body of Confederate cavalry. In the ensuing battle, Stuart was mortally wounded, but Sheridan's threat to the Confederate capital ended when he ordered a withdrawal to Union lines that evening.

On May 12, Major General J.E.B. Stuart, the great cavalry commander, died from his wound. With all Confederate forces engaged in actions above and below Richmond, there was no funeral procession such as that with Stonewall Jackson a year earlier. In fact, barely a corporal's guard was available to escort Stuart's body to the grave. Robert E. Lee, with his army at Spotsylvania, learned of Stuart's death via a dispatch from Richmond.

Upon reading it, Lee announced Stuart's loss to those in his presence and added, "He never brought me a piece of false information."[115] This profound statement clearly showed how much Lee trusted and relied on Stuart for military intelligence, and Hampton's Scouts provided much of it.

Stuart's death came just a week after Lee's senior infantry corps commander, General James Longstreet, was wounded in a friendly fire incident, keeping him from field duty until October. The question of who would succeed Stuart was not immediately answered, and Generals Wade Hampton, Fitzhugh Lee and Rooney Lee, Stuart's division commanders, reported directly to Robert E. Lee. But these were matters beyond the Scouts, who continued to do their duty.

By the middle of May, the old Scouts from South Carolina arrived unmounted and wasted no time in obtaining horses by taking vulnerable Yankee picket posts. The earliest recorded date of their deployment is May 26, when Jim Guffin, Bernard King, Walker Russell and Wallace Miller were together on a patrol.[116] The return of these men must have felt like a godsend to Shadburne.

With Meade's army locked in deadly battle with Lee's infantry, Hampton's Scouts were assigned to cover the Confederate left flank for the detection of any Union movements from that direction. Still behind Union lines but in a much smaller area, the Scouts concentrated their efforts on aggressive patrolling. These patrols resulted in little sleep and broken rest, but the men were undeterred in fulfilling their duties. At the end of May, the opposing armies were licking their wounds and preparing for the next engagement. The Iron Scouts, back up to full strength, felt confident and prepared for another month of close contact with the enemy.

JUNE 1864

I n early June, Colonel Fred Waring, commanding the Jeff Davis Legion, wrote in his journal, "The Scouts report that Sheridan is preparing for a raid. He was dissatisfied with his last."[117] A few days later, Scouts Hugh Scott and Adolphus Kennedy left Confederate lines, heading to the north side of the Anna River, but happened across Sheridan and nearly ten thousand Yankees crossing the Pamunkey River with many wagons and artillery pieces. Scott and Kennedy reached a bluff, giving them a clear view of the enemy, and counted regimental flags and artillery pieces. Kennedy then returned to Hampton's headquarters, a distance of about thirty-five miles, and gave a report. Scott watched the Yankee camp that night and verified the road they took before heading to Hampton with a follow-up report.[118]

Additional reports on this massive Union force came to Hampton from other Scouts that day. Hampton correctly determined that Sheridan was heading west to Charlottesville to meet up with another Union army under General David Hunter and destroy valuable railroad facilities at Gordonsville and elsewhere. On June 9, well before sunrise, Hampton set out with his division and that of Fitzhugh Lee, about 6,400 men in all, with a plan to intercept Sheridan at Trevilian Station, just east of Gordonsville. Shadburne and his men tracked Sheridan's force nearly every step of the way, keeping Hampton fully apprised of Sheridan's progress.

On June 11, the two forces collided in the largest all-cavalry battle in U.S. history. Hampton, though substantially outnumbered, stopped Sheridan's advance and forced him to begin a retreat the night of June 12. Hampton followed the next day in hot pursuit, but Sheridan declined to face Hampton in battle again. Hampton tried every way he could during the next eleven days to force another battle with Sheridan—intending to destroy him completely—but Sheridan managed to escape Hampton's clutches and re-joined Meade's army. However, on June 24, Hampton crushed a Union force under General Gregg at Samaria Church. Scouts Dick Hogan, Wallace Miller and Daniel Cloud, a Virginia Scout from the Seventh Virginia Cavalry, distinguished themselves by guiding Confederate troops to a position where they hit Gregg's flank and routed his command.[119]

During the lengthy pursuit of Sheridan's force, Shadburne and his Scouts remained in the saddle day and night tracking Sheridan's progress, taking prisoners and engaging in small firefights. Hugh Scott, after one long night's vigil, sought breakfast at a farmhouse. Arriving from the back side, he spotted about ten Yankees in the yard and another two in the barn. He wrote, "I put spurs to my horse and charged and yelled, 'Come on boys, here they are'…I had a double barrel shotgun, and I shot two from their horses and captured two, and brought away four horses."[120] The others fled without hesitation. Scott didn't say if he got his breakfast.

Members of Hampton's command didn't get to savor the victories for long because they were quickly called on to respond to another Union cavalry raid. Generals August Kautz and James Wilson led about 5,500 men backed with ample artillery on a mission designed to destroy Confederate railroads as far west as Staunton River Bridge at Roanoke Station. They successfully burned several railway stations and tore up about sixty miles of track before being forced to turn toward friendly lines after being defeated by a small Confederate force at Staunton River Bridge. Hampton, forewarned of their route, attacked them at Sappony Church on June 28 and forced them northward to Ream's Station, where, the next day, he again attacked, this time with infantry supporting his cavalry. The Yankee generals abandoned their artillery, burned their wagons full of supplies and stolen loot and broke into smaller groups while attempting to reach Union lines just a few miles away.[121] The raid, though moderately successful to this point, ended in a complete rout by Confederate forces.

Hampton's Scouts were deeply involved in both closing actions with notable service, but Sergeant Shadburne's exploits at Ream's Station were extraordinary. At one point, he was riding alone through a forest trying to locate the enemy when he came to a road. Describing the scene, he wrote, "The road was packed with the enemy, every vestige of booty gone, some mounted, many unmounted, all fleeing in wildest confusion to, they knew not where, anywhere to get away from the hated rebels."[122] Shadburne charged the nearest group and "commanded surrender, which they willingly did and [Shadburne] marched seventeen of them, still heavily armed…to General Butler."[123]

Having turned the prisoners over to a guard, Shadburne returned to the woods, headed for the road again, but this time with six other Scouts. Sighting a large mounted enemy force on the road, Shadburne left the woods alone and blocked their advance. Commanding them to surrender, he identified himself as a general with a substantial force, including Mosby, in the woods around them. When the Union riders hesitated, Shadburne called for his compatriots to join him in the road. There, they formed alongside him with revolvers drawn. When Shadburne threatened to open fire, the enemy force responded with a surrender.

This magnificent bluff captured the entire eighty-man advance guard of General Wilson. Shadburne identified the six with him as Scouts James Sloan, Wallace Miller, Dan Tanner, Shakespeare Harris, William Rife and one other man whose name is lost to memory. In a postwar letter, Shadburne claimed that this was one of his greatest personal adventures and won him a captaincy.[124]

The Scouts spent nearly every day in the saddle or in combat during the month of June. Hampton gave the Scouts well-deserved credit in his after-action report covering operations of June 27–30.[125] Their reports, as always, were timely, accurate and invaluable in helping propel the Southern cavalry to these latest notable successes.

July–August 1864

With the heavy campaigning of June complete, the Scouts and the rest of the Confederate cavalry found themselves in an entirely different situation in early July. Meade's Army of the Potomac crossed the James River and invested Petersburg in mid-June during the Battle of Trevilian Station and subsequent pursuit by Hampton. With the opposing armies settling in with fortifications and trenches, the flurry and movements of a campaign slowed down sufficiently to allow the cavalry, newly posted below Petersburg, to rest horses and recover from the intensity of the action-packed month of June.

The Scouts had little time to rest, for theirs was a never-ending mission and they were now facing substantial challenges beyond the ordinary. Their area of operations abruptly shifted from northern Virginia to a vast expanse from Petersburg bounded by the James River to Norfolk to the east and southward by the railroad line leading to Weldon, North Carolina. It differed in every possible way from northern Virginia because of the terrain. Low, swampy areas, sluggish rivers and streams bordered by dense forests with few roads or open fields required the Scouts to make substantial procedural changes in adapting to their new environment. With few pockets of civilization and mostly scattered farms in this zone of operations, the Scouts could not depend on friendly civilians on a regular basis. Residents with Unionist leanings were identified and avoided as much as possible.

Much of July was spent exploring this new ground and determining how best to solve certain logistical worries. Private John Elliott, in a postwar

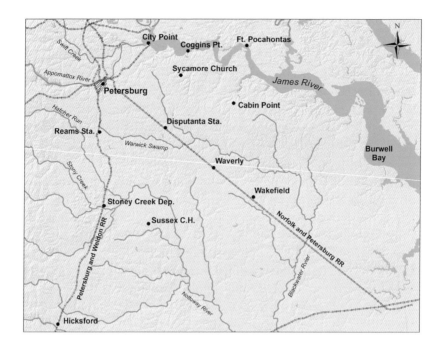

Operational area of Hampton's Scouts, July 1864–April 1865. *Courtesy of Scott Williams and the Chesterfield Historical Society of Virginia.*

article relating his scouting experiences, described the situation: "I had quite an extensive territory, expanding from the Petersburg & Weldon Railroad, to the James River. It required some time to gain a knowledge of the country, its topography and people before we could make our plans to the best advantage."[126]

The Scouts were on their own in locating sites for rest and assembly, foraging for their horses, obtaining sustenance for themselves, determining suitable routes for scouting the area, finding entrance and egress points through the Union lines and a multitude of other concerns. Shadburne, Hogan and the others resolved these daunting problems quickly and efficiently. Too much credit cannot be given them for the energy, thought and resourcefulness needed in overcoming these gargantuan challenges in a manner allowing them to resume their primary duties behind the enemy lines in less than two weeks.

The records are unclear, but the Scouts seem to have established multiple camps throughout the swamps and deep in forests where they felt the Yankees would fear to venture. They used a series of small sites as camps of convenience and assembly points throughout the region as well. Further, they established strong relationships with a small number of friendly civilians.

The earliest confirmed mention found of the Scouts in position behind Meade's army in July is from Colonel Waring's diary. On July 19, he entered, "Saw Shadburne. He talks very coolly of having killed several Yankees."[127] However, one day earlier, Major General Philip Sheridan, commander of the Cavalry Corps of the Army of the Potomac, sent the following message to Meade's chief of staff: "There are about fifteen or twenty guerrillas in the vicinity of Sycamore Church. They are dismounted, and have several times fired on my pickets at that church today, killing 1 officer, wounding 1 man and 1 of my couriers. Can I have permission to burn a few houses down in that neighborhood?"[128]

Meade's response granted Sheridan permission to do so, but only under very strict conditions: "In giving this [limited] authority the commanding general wishes to avoid punishing innocent parties who may not have it in their power to prevent the offenses being committed."[129]

The guerrillas mentioned by Sheridan were likely Hampton's Scouts. Another group, the Signal Corps Scouts, were active but generally stayed near the James River and farther east than the Sycamore Church. With a standing strength of about thirty men, the Signal Corps's scouts regularly engaged Union patrols far away from Shadburne and his men. Regardless, the *Official Records* chronicle the problems of the Union cavalry in dealing with Confederates behind the lines from July 1864 into early 1865. Pickets, couriers and videttes were taken most nights, prompting frustration, arguments and finger-pointing by senior Union officers. Some Union reports stated that the culprits were merely dismounted Confederate cavalrymen seeking horses. This was only partly true, for Hampton's Scouts were heavily involved.

Shadburne and his men were in high gear by late July. Colonel Waring's diary makes mention of two Scouts in his entry of July 28. He wrote, "[Private Walter] Ashby returned from Suffolk this morning and says that the Yankees have taken almost all the horses in that quarter. Ladies ride in vehicles drawn by a single ox."[130] He added, "[Private John] Elliott returned & says that the expedition designed to cut off the party we heard of will not pay. The Yankees are picketing very closely. They keep out chains of pickets."[131] On August 4, Waring made another brief note about the Scouts: "Ashby & Williams were sent out last night on a scout."[132] The next day, he wrote, "Saw a Yankee sergt [prisoner of war] who informed us that Torbert's [Union cavalry general Alfred T.A. Torbert] division had left City Point in transports….A scout informed Gen Lee that 45 transports had gone down the river which were loaded with cavalry."[133] It is abundantly clear, then, that Shadburne's men were spread widely over their assigned area of responsibility and successfully performing a variety of tasks.

The Scouts continued their work at a high level into August, providing Lee with regular updates on the activities of the vast Union army while taking prisoners and much needed horses and equipment. Despite the obstacles facing them, they seem to have avoided suffering any casualties in their incursions and roamed freely on their missions. Union efforts to block them were relatively ineffective, particularly considering the effort made. General A.V. Kautz wrote that his entire division was on duty—mainly picketing and patrolling—leaving him no reserves. He added, "Six of my men have been captured in the past six days on this line in spite of every precaution to prevent them."[134] General David Gregg reported, "[A]ll quiet on the cavalry picket line from the James River to the left of the Fifth Army Corps. General Kautz reports one man…slightly wounded and another captured, with horse and equipment, by guerrillas last night while on picket."[135]

One particular event in August was joyfully received not only by the Scouts, but nearly the entire cavalry corps of the Army of Northern Virginia. This moment of jubilation was the August 11 announcement that Major-General Wade Hampton was named commander of Lee's cavalry. Hampton was a proven leader, field general and tactician respected by those serving under him. His selection as Stuart's successor was widely acclaimed in all quarters. Brigadier General Matthew C. Butler succeeded Hampton as division commander, and Hampton's Division was renamed Butler's Division. Butler was promoted to major general in September.

These changes also filtered down to Hampton's Scouts. On paper, at least, the Scouts were divided into two groups. One was led by Shadburne, who remained chief of scouts for Hampton. Dick Hogan, named chief of scouts for Butler, led the other. In reality, there was negligible change in operations. Multiple accounts show them acting as one command in tandem or intermingled. It is apparent that the personal friendship and respect shared by Shadburne and Hogan prevented jealousy, squabbles or other conflict from interfering with the good order and missions of the Scouts. This remarkable pairing shows the high personal and professional

Postwar photograph of Major General Matthew C. Butler, CSA. *Library of Congress.*

qualities of each man and reflects the high level of dedication within the Scouts organization.

The Scouts remained busy and vigilant through August. Working in small teams, they covered substantial ground in a single day, but encounters with enemy patrols were common. The depth of trust and respect they enjoyed from their senior cavalry officers is well illustrated in an account by one Scout, Private John Elliott of the Jeff Davis Legion, who wrote, "I applied to Hampton for forty well mounted and armed men to attack one of these persistent and adventurous patrol parties that had given us a great deal of trouble.…They had boasted to the citizens that they intended to have us dead or alive.…The men asked for were furnished."[136]

Elliott and his party devised a plan intended to annihilate this threat by preparing an elaborate ambush. He wrote:

> We hauled down about a half mile of telegraph wire…rolled it into small bundles, and carried it six or eight miles and during the night formed the ambush. We stretched the wire across the road just high enough to catch a man above the saddle [and] wound it around trees to secure it. This was done at the head of a long cut in the road and extending it more than a hundred yards back on each side.… [W]e made the wire pretty much like a partridge net.[137]

Carried out flawlessly on a bright Sunday morning, Elliott, with perhaps ten other Scouts reinforced by the forty-man contingent provided by Hampton, caught the Union command by total surprise, creating a mad panic. Elliott wrote, "The Federal column broke in an instant, the rear half flying for dear life. We closed in on the others and such a scramble was rarely seen during the war."[138] He added, "They went with such force against the wire that it broke and most of them escaped."[139] The ambush still resulted in numerous losses to the Yankees while emphatically conveying the message that Hampton's Scouts could strike anywhere at any time.

This was just one of many actions in August involving Union cavalry and the Scouts. Elliott clearly defined the situation: "We soon made a hazardous business for the enemy to scout outside his lines with anything less than one hundred men well mounted and armed. Fight after fight took place between us and these small parties for more than a month.… Disputana Station, on the Petersburg and Norfolk Railroad, was the scene and battleground of some of the most persistent of these hand-to-hand fights. The enemy soon became more cautious and we became bolder and more daring going into Federal lines and capturing a few pickets as we came out."[140]

On August 11, the same day he was named Jeb Stuart's successor, Wade Hampton led a substantial portion of his cavalry to Culpepper, Virginia, to counter anticipated Union moves in the Shenandoah Valley. Shortly after his departure, the Scouts detected preparations for a new Union offensive toward Richmond. On August 13, a substantial Union force crossed the James River on a pontoon bridge with hopes of taking Richmond. The next day, Hampton was ordered to join the Confederate forces facing this new threat, which developed into the Second Battle of Deep Bottom. It appears Hampton sent for Sergeant Shadburne and some of his Scouts to meet him in Richmond, for there is concrete evidence Shadburne and seven other Scouts received forage for their horses in that city on August 14 and 15.[141] There could be no reason other than a summons by Hampton to explain the presence of such a large contingent of Scouts in Richmond at this time.

Hampton and his cavalry played pivotal roles in the heavy fighting at Deep Bottom and earned acclaim from all quarters for their contributions to the battlefield success. The week-long action ended only when Union forces withdrew from the field on the night of August 20. What roles Shadburne and his Scouts played during the battle are unknown, but the fact Hampton wanted them there was a sure sign of how much he depended on them.

The month of August was far from over for the Scouts. Those remaining below Petersburg detected another Union offensive even while the Second Battle of Deep Bottom was raging. On August 18, a strong Union force moved out with intentions of taking Globe Station on the vital Weldon Railroad. It succeeded on the twenty-first and began tearing up track southward heading to Ream's Station. Hampton returned to face this new threat on August 23. He quickly devised a plan in which his cavalry and A.P. Hill's infantry could stop the enemy advance and destruction of the railroad before it reached Ream's Station. The plan was wildly successful and ended with a complete rout of the Union forces in the Second Battle of Reams Station on the twenty-fifth. Again, Hampton's cavalry was lauded for its battlefield contributions. Unfortunately, the Yankees still held Globe Tavern, a key portion of the Weldon Railroad, thereby hampering delivery of supplies to Lee's army until the war's end. While the Scouts certainly detected the enemy movements leading to Globe Tavern and Ream's Station, no written accounts of their involvement in these battles are known.

In late August, new names were added to the Scout roster. Private W.H. "Bill" Turner of the Sixth South Carolina Cavalry and Private Dan Tanner of Cobb's Legion were appointed Scouts.[142] These were "good times" for Hampton's Scouts, and their successes were piling up.

SEPTEMBER 1864

One late August night, shortly after the fighting at Ream's Station, Sergeant Shadburne and Private John Elliott were on patrol together behind the enemy lines not far from the headquarters of General U.S. Grant at City Point. What they discovered that fateful night set in motion one of the most successful and audacious cavalry raids of the entire war. Just before daybreak, they noticed a large herd of cattle, but the heavy presence of guards forced the two Scouts to pull back before they could check it out. That night, they returned with fellow Scouts Shakespeare Harris and Rufus Merchant. Leaving their horses about a mile from the Union pickets, they advanced cautiously on foot to the site. There they split up, with Shadburne and Merchant going to one side of the pasture while Elliott and Harris went to the other. After an all-night reconnaissance, the intrepid troopers passed through the Union pickets, returned to their horses and compared notes. They had actually located two large cattle herds that had been moved to Coggins Point on August 29 and were protected by pickets and roving patrols. Leaving his companions to rest and sleep, Shadburne rode to Hampton's headquarters, a fifty-mile trip, to advise him of the cattle. Upon returning the next evening, Shadburne reported that Hampton would inform Robert E. Lee of the herds and wanted the Scouts to continue monitoring the cattle closely.[143]

No other records exist of Shadburne's communications with Hampton, but obviously, each man recognized the possibility of capturing the cattle right from under Grant's nose. The seeds were planted, and for the next couple of weeks, Hampton's Scouts maintained constant vigilance on the cattle while curtailing their other activities in the vicinity so as to not attract additional Union pickets or patrols.[144]

The earliest known written reference to the possibility of taking Grant's cattle is from Shadburne in a very detailed and lengthy September 5 dispatch delivered to Hampton via Dick Hogan. This message provided the complete disposition of Union forces in such a precisely detailed manner that it became the basis of later planning. The scope of information within it clearly indicates substantial efforts were expended by Shadburne and his men over a few short days and nights. It also shows Shadburne and Hampton had previously discussed the possibility of a raid in some detail.[145]

Hampton put forth a formal plan to Robert E. Lee three days later, and Lee responded in a dispatch dated September 9. While adding a couple of suggestions to Hampton's proposal, Lee authorized Hampton to carry out his plan. In his remarks pertaining to the return phase of the raid, Lee wrote, "Let your movement depend upon the reports of your scouts."[146] This telling statement adds confirmation to the degree of Lee's awareness of Hampton's Scouts and their capabilities as well as the trust he had in them to execute their responsibilities.

In the early morning hours of September 15, Hampton put his cavalry in motion. The three-thousand-man contingent was divided into three parties guided by Hampton's Scouts, including Shadburne and Hogan. Numerous Scouts rode on the flanks or ahead along the routes to be taken to ensure security and provide warning if enemy patrols were detected. Hampton's orders were carried out flawlessly and, upon reaching the cattle site the following day, he found the enemy totally unaware of his movements.

Hampton began his attack at 5:00 a.m. on September 16. He personally granted the thirteen Scouts assembled with him the honor of leading the attack, and after an intense but short mêlée, the cattle were in Confederate hands. Unfortunately, the Scouts suffered several casualties. Sergeant James McCalla was the lone fatality. One witness later wrote, "Just before he breathed his last General Hampton rode up to where he lay, dismounted, took him in his arms, and, weeping over him, said: 'McCaula [McCalla], I will tell your people how you fought this day.' And the poor fellow, much comforted, smiled, and died in peace."[147]

Other casualties included Hugh Scott, who was shot in the wrist, and Walker Russell, who was hurt when knocked off his horse by an enemy rifle butt. One other unidentified Scout was wounded.[148] Despite the expedition's success, the loss of four Scouts in a single day stung.

The return trip to Confederate lines was conducted flawlessly, without any cattle being lost. Hampton's entire command, with the cattle, were within Confederate lines the morning of September 17, leading to great jubilation all across the South and tremendous embarrassment to Grant and his generals. The raid became known as Hampton's Great Beefsteak Raid, and Shadburne's name was prominently mentioned in dispatches and newspaper accounts. The raid netted almost 2,500 cattle and over three hundred prisoners, while Confederate casualties were about sixty men. Hampton's report of the raid, dated September 27, gave prominent mention to his Scouts:

> *I cannot close my report without notice of the conduct of the scouts with me. Sergeant Shadburne, of the Jeff. Davis Legion, who gave me the information about the cattle, acted as guide to General Rosser, accompanied the regiment in its charge, kept his party always in the front, and acted with conspicuous gallantry. Sergeant Hogan, in charge of Butler's scouts, also displayed great activity, intelligence, and boldness. Of the scouts, Sergeant McCalla,…a most valuable man, was killed and three others wounded.*[149]

September 1864 was a banner month for Hampton's Scouts in other respects. Besides the Beefsteak Raid, their other activities wreaked havoc on Yankee pickets and patrols in an almost nonstop pace. One of the more notable events began on September 2, when Hugh Scott and a few others on patrol stole into a Union camp and rode seven horses out without being detected—not an easy task at all.[150] The next day, Scott and fellow scout Jim Niblet barely escaped a Union ambush, in which Niblet was shot in three places. Scott managed to extricate Niblet and himself from the scene and sought Dick Hogan, who was close by. With intentions of catching the ambush party, Hogan led a squad of Scouts on foot through woods toward a road, seeking the enemy force. However, upon reaching the road, they unexpectedly encountered, and quickly captured, two Yankee supply wagons, their drivers and three guards. The small party immediately re-entered the woods to take their prisoners, wagons and horses in, but before going far, they realized an enemy cavalry force was behind them in pursuit. Undaunted, Hogan sent the prisoners forward and quickly set up an ambush. Hugh Scott wrote, "We…killed and captured every one of the whole twenty-five men right there."[151] A preliminary Union account confirms the essence of this action and states that after capture of the wagons, "A force was sent in pursuit that came upon the enemy in superior force and there was a severe fight."[152] This initial report admitted to one dead and four wounded, but the totals almost certainly were increased in later reports. In the end, Hogan and his men took numerous prisoners, killed or wounded others and brought in eight fine mules, two wagons with supplies and critically needed leather harnesses and other goods for which the Confederate Quartermaster Corps must have been quite grateful.

Union commanders reacted to the constant loss of pickets with deep levels of frustration and anger. On September 5, standing orders were given that those responsible "if captured, should not be sent in as prisoners."[153] A flurry of other substantial and extreme efforts were ordered or designed to rid themselves of the stings inflicted by the Scouts and others below Petersburg.[154]

October–November 1864

The first of October found Hampton's Scouts' roster at its height. Late September brought several more permanent Scouts by appointments for Privates Joel Adams, Phil Hutchinson and Solomon Legare of the Sixth South Carolina Cavalry; William W. Rife of the Jeff Davis Legion; and William M. Waterbury of the Third North Carolina Cavalry.[155] A couple of other men, Privates F.M. McClure and N.B. Eison, from the Sixth and Fifth South Carolina, respectively, were quite active and are found in various accounts. It is uncertain if they were detached or serving as occasional Scouts. One other man, Private John C. Colvin, was on the roster and served well. Oddly, no service records of any sort exist for him. His postwar statements and obituary omit when, or even if, he had ever formally joined a regiment. Available details indicate that Colvin, a young Virginian from Prince William County who lost three brothers fighting for the South in the war, became a member of the Scouts because of his value in northern Virginia while still a civilian. His affiliation date with them is unknown, but he is first mentioned in accounts as being one of the Scouts involved in Hampton's Beefsteak Raid. However, in a postwar statement, he claimed service from 1863.[156] Despite the unusual circumstances, Colvin was said to be a brave and efficient member of the Scouts.

With a total of thirty detached men plus several occasional Scouts, Shadburne and Hogan now had squads sized to cover more ground on a quicker basis. Additionally, they now had the opportunity to form larger strike forces when needed to counter the ever-increasing threats of Union patrols.

A Union report dated October 12 states that fourteen Confederate prisoners were received by Meade's provost marshal and claimed, "Four of them are regularly detailed scouts belonging to General Butler's division of cavalry."[157] Confederate records show only two of Hampton's Scouts were captured. Privates W.W Russell and Dolph Kennedy (First and Second South Carolina, respectively) were taken together on October 11 when returning from an extended mission to Norfolk "to locate the position of General Dix, who commanded that department of Virginia."[158] Notations on their individual capture records read in part, "[He is a] Scout and has been hovering around our rear. Should be held until such time as that the information he may be possessed of will do no injury to our army."[159]

Though a relatively quiet month, the Scouts maintained a high level of activity. Colonel Fred Waring, commander of the Jeff Davis Legion, made several entries in his daily journal regarding the Scouts. Walter Ashby, John Elliott and John Chapman were dispatched together on October 19 on an unidentified special mission.[160] In his entry of October 29, Waring noted, "[William H.] Hoard [Hord] reported today. He and 3 others went along the Yankee line of pickets and relieved four of their horses."[161]

November was a different story, and not all of it was good. In many ways, this month reflects the coming together of Union efforts to thwart the Scouts in their activities, with six Scouts being made prisoner. Solomon Legare and Shakespeare Harris were captured together on November 7 when, with Shadburne and Jim Sloan, a Union force surprised them while eating breakfast at the house of a friendly citizen. The four Scouts fled toward the nearby woods amid a hail of bullets and the Union commander shouting orders to his men to take no prisoners. Legare was shot in the ankle before going far, but when the others reached a fence line, they turned on their attackers. Harris described the scene: "Shadburne yelled, defiantly, 'Boys, give them hell.' We levelled our double-barreled shotguns and fired, and seven of them reeled and leaped like bullfrogs from their horses….They soon rallied and came at us again. We fired and three more fell."[162]

The Yankees kept coming, and in the ensuing action, Harris took bullets to an arm and a leg and received a saber wound to his neck. Shadburne was shot in the neck, and it looked like the entire lot of Scouts was to be killed or captured. Harris remembered that "a federal soldier was about to brain [Shadburne] with the butt end of a gun, Sloan reached up from the ground and shot him through the stomach….Sloan dragged wounded Shadburne into the woods, and the [Yankee] detachment, fearing an ambuscade, pursued no further."[163]

Wartime sketch of a Union vidette, a favorite target of Hampton's Scouts. *Library of Congress.*

Sloan and Shadburne made good their escape, but Harris and Legare were taken prisoner despite the orders given by the Federal commander. Yet they were not out of danger. Harris wrote, "Legare and myself were taken to prison....Hampton through Lee sent a flag of truce to say that we were both enlisted soldiers, else we would soon have been executed as marauders or spies."[164] This is the only instance known of Scouts facing threats of execution after being captured. It is also typical of Hampton to take extraordinary measures to protect his men.

The losses mounted, with the capture of Wallace Miller on the fifteenth, William Waterbury on the nineteenth, Bill Turner on the twenty-eighth and Tom Thistle on the thirtieth.[165] However, these losses did not substantially diminish overall activities of the Scouts in November. Colonel Waring's journal entry for November 10 mentions that Private John S. Elliott and others were preparing a trap for the Yankees. On Saturday, November 12, he mentioned two other Scouts: "[William W.] Rife sent me a pistol just captured from the Yankees with a very pretty note. Phil Hutchinson brought it to me."[166]

Scene of large Union picket post. Such posts were frequently taken by Hampton's Scouts. *Library of Congress.*

The *Richmond Daily Dispatch* carried an article on November 15 that read:

> *Three of General Hampton's scouts have just performed a very handsome exploit. Last Thursday* [November 10] *they penetrated to the neighborhood of Fort Powhatan, on the James River, below City Point, and attacked and captured twenty-six Yankees, belonging to the Army of the James, who were foraging on the south side. They succeeded in reaching General Hampton's headquarters with twenty-three of the prisoners, three of them having escaped on the way.*[167]

Nothing pertaining to this remarkable accomplishment is found elsewhere, and the intrepid individual Scouts who carried it out remain unidentified. Bringing this many prisoners to Confederate lines was a challenge, for it required a trip of about sixty miles from point of capture, most of which was regularly patrolled by Union cavalry.

Colonel Waring's journal entry of November 22 makes mention of another request for regular cavalry to support an operation of the Scouts. "Rode over to see Gen. [Matthew C.] Butler. He wants Elliot to go out with 50 men to ambuscade the Yankees near Nance's Shop. I consented to let him have some of my dismounted men."[168] It is interesting that Private Elliott was directly involved in arranging two separate ambushes within an interval of just twelve days. What, if anything, came from them is unknown. These are the second and third substantial ambushes that he is known to have planned.

On November 29, Shadburne and twelve other Scouts were using a private residence belonging to a Mrs. Tatum below Petersburg as temporary headquarters, with each man having two horses there. Their day began before sunup, when the Scouts awoke, fed and saddled their horses and sat down for breakfast. Midway through their meal, they were alerted to the presence of a sizeable Union cavalry force in the act of surrounding the house.

Shadburne led his men out the front door, and they charged the enemy, killing several. Cut off from the stables holding their horses, the Scouts were forced to flee in haste on foot across open fields. Shadburne called for a halt after being chased for several hundred yards and said, "Get in line, men, or they will capture every one of us. Let's fight it out."[169] With his men rallied, they spread out ready for close action with a much larger force. Their determined stand and good shooting repulsed two assaults by their foe. When the Yankees fell back to regroup, the Scouts seized the opportunity to continue their flight to the woods. Somehow along the way, Shadburne was captured, but he quickly escaped from his guards amid a hail of gunfire and rejoined his companions in the woods, where they stayed until the Yankees left.[170]

Returning to the house, they learned the enemy had carried off their horses but had suffered twenty-six dead and wounded.[171] Now on foot, the Scouts walked nearly twenty miles to a Yankee picket post. Hugh Scott wrote, "We went down that night, and killed nine men and captured seventeen gray horses, then we went on up to the general place of rendezvous and camped in the woods and pitched our little tents."[172]

The next morning, their camp was discovered by the Yankees, Tom Thistle was captured and they lost all but seven of their horses. Hugh Scott described the scene: "We were to meet a Virginia [scouting] party.…Before day we heard a rumbling through the woods. Everybody was up but one of the Scouts, Dr. Tom Thistle, a surgeon. We could not get him up. He said, 'That is [the Virginia scouting] party' but it was the Yankees. They… captured Dr. Tom Thistle."[173]

Undaunted after their second narrow escape in two days, they trekked to the site of another Union picket post. Hugh Scott succinctly described what followed: "That night we went to another end of the line, where there were twenty-one men on post. We laid down and crawled up to them, I suppose in fifteen steps of them.…We charged them on foot and brought away twenty-one horses and killed sixteen or seventeen men."[174]

Those last two days of November must have struck fear into the Union cavalry commanders. The Scouts had virtually wiped out two sizeable, widely separated picket posts and not only escaped from but also soundly whipped a much larger force sent to catch them. Over fifty Union soldiers were killed or wounded in the three engagements, while the Scouts lost just one man to capture.

December 1864

Despite the bitterly cold weather, the opposing armies had moments of intense activity in December, but little of the Scouts' activity is recorded. There simply is nothing relating to their activities except for a period early in the month in which Union forces, led by General Gouverneur Warren, attempted to destroy the Petersburg and Weldon Railroad at Hicksford (now Emporia), Virginia. Called Warren's Weldon Raid by some, it is better known as the Applejack Raid.

This marginally successful expedition is generally seen as just another of the multiple moves below Petersburg by Meade's army in 1864. It was far more than that to the Scouts, for they found themselves drawn into unimagined conditions far beyond the normal horrors of war. The shameful and contemptible depredations perpetrated on civilians in Warren's path, similar to Sherman's march across Georgia and Sheridan's destruction in the Shenandoah Valley, were foreign to their eyes and experiences.

Though the expedition officially began December 7, Hampton and Lee had been alerted several days earlier by reports from Sergeant Shadburne that Warren's corps was making ready for a movement.[175] Writing in the third person, Shadburne wrote, "The writer for several dark and tempestuous nights…had been 'in the lines' and saw the enemy were unusually active for that season of the year. Rations for many days were being cooked, wagons were being loaded, arms and accoutrements were gotten into readiness and a general stir was prevalent."[176]

As Warren's force of about twenty-seven thousand men began its march, two horsemen wearing Union uniforms rode unnoticed along its length. Shadburne was one of them and wrote about that morning ride in his peculiar style:

> *That morning Shadburne and Isaac Curtis, of General W.H.F. Lee's command (in blue), rode through the enemy's column, commanding the stragglers to "close up" and Shadburne reported to General Hampton, "That Warren's destination was doubtless Weldon."…Then he hastily returned alone, again passing through Warren's line of march, and assembled his scouts, about 20 men.*[177]

The route used by Warren's force was virtually untouched by the war. Farmers had enjoyed a bountiful autumn harvest. Their livestock, chickens and sheep were plentiful, and some had cotton bales ready for market. They also had large quantities of applejack, a particularly flavorful fermented home brew with substantial alcoholic content. The very first day resulted in such massive straggling from the Union force that three companies of cavalry were detached to round up as many of these roamers as could be found and return them to Petersburg. About 850 of Warren's men were collected that day and returned, but other Union soldiers invaded houses and barnyards, taking whatever pleased them.[178] Mutton, fresh beef and chicken were a common camp supper that night for the Yankee army and was often washed down by massive quantities of stolen applejack. This was a common theme throughout the expedition.[179] Union accounts claim that they burned only a few houses and outbuildings as they passed through but ignore the other outrages that occurred in this near pristine part of Virginia.[180]

Hampton's Scouts trailed Warren's force, sending regular reports to Generals Hampton and Butler. Shadburne wrote, "Our ambition was to harass and destroy the enemy's rear, and we did it quite satisfactorily."[181] They encountered some stragglers and made them prisoners, but as they rode on and recognized what was happening to the countryside, this practice was abandoned. Shadburne wrote, "Fast and furious became our charges and each time many of the enemy told no tales; prisoners we did not want."[182]

They saw firsthand the results of home intrusions from the stragglers and felt the frustration of near helplessness of doing anything about it. Incensed at the outrages against the civilians, the Scouts rode with a purpose. In the afternoon, they happened upon a house and learned that a sizeable Union infantry force had just departed after looting the property and raping the female inhabitant. Seeing the villains on the road not far away, Shadburne led his men in a charge on the unsuspecting Yankees:

> *That charge left that company of New York Zouaves to tell no tales; their lust for booty and beauty doubtless gave them to the devil. The sequel to this occurrence was that when the infernal vandals returned…they burned this poor woman's home; first they robbed her of woman's proudest inheritance, then they stripped her of her house and turned her out in the pitiless storm.*[183]

On December 9, General Warren gave the order to return to Union lines at Petersburg. Having to be satisfied with tearing up about fifteen miles of the railroad, his decision was influenced by learning sizeable Confederate forces under Generals A.P. Hill and Wade Hampton were moving on him. Additionally, there were substantial doubts that any attempt to cross the Meherrin River at Hicksford, stoutly defended by a small Confederate force, would be successful.

What little restraint his men had shown regarding civilians earlier was entirely absent on the return trip. As they retraced their rout, numerous dead Union soldiers were found in Sussex County. When rumors, true or not, spread that the bodies were stripped and mutilated, the Yankees took vengeance on the local citizens. Some were murdered, while widespread looting and pillaging took place.[184] One Union post-action report admitted that "the burning of buildings commenced, in retaliation, and nearly every building, including the Sussex courthouse, for miles, was given to flames."[185] Hampton's Scouts reported these events and received instructions "that when they caught Yankees in the act of robbing and burning to take the vandals by the arms and legs and swing them in the flames, drunk or sober."[186]

Warren's command reached Union lines on December 12. Casualties sustained in the expedition were not fully reported by Union commanders. That the Scouts captured some and killed a substantial number of others is certain, but no figures are found anywhere. The raid was a wretched affair in that it left an indelible stain of dishonor and disgrace on the Union army.[187]

14

January–April 1865 (Virginia)

Scout activities following the Applejack Raid in early December until early January 1865 are unknown. Nothing is found pertaining to their operations in postwar accounts, *Official Records* or newspapers. Undoubtedly, they were at work concentrating on their endless missions but whatever successes gained or challenges encountered have gone unrecorded.

January, however, did become a milestone month for Hampton, for he received orders to return to South Carolina with two brigades of Matthew C. Butler's division, as a temporary measure, to assist in fighting General William T. Sherman, who had entered South Carolina from Georgia. All the South Carolina Scouts were recalled to their regiments and soon departed Virginia. Hampton departed Virginia on January 22, three days after his various commands began leaving.

This sudden undertaking affected one of the most valuable resources of the Army of Northern Virginia. The success of Hampton's Scouts over the previous two years was nothing short of stunning and distinguished, and it seems odd that Robert E. Lee would allow them to be interfered with in any way at this stage of the war. Fortunately for Lee, for unexplained reasons, Sergeant Shadburne and a handful of Scouts from the Jeff Davis Legion remained in Virginia, even though their regiment was sent to South Carolina.[189] Some of those remaining are identified by Shadburne in a postwar account as Dan Tanner, John H. McIlwayne, William W. Rife and Archibald Waller. They were supported by reliable James Sloan of the First North Carolina Cavalry. There may have been others, but nothing is found identifying them.[189] Losing the main part of such an experienced and smooth-running detachment would ordinarily spell disaster, but that did not occur.

Sergeant Shadburne was blessed to have had those well-seasoned veterans volunteering to remain with him. Their action speaks volumes about the trust and respect given him and reflects favorably on their own personal honor and courage. Shadburne secured a few more men to ride with him from elsewhere, but their names or regiments are not found. Technically, they could still be called Hampton's Scouts because the War Department had authorized Hampton and his cavalry to be away from Virginia for only a few months. One newspaper article, for unknown reasons, called them "Shadburne's Scouts." What they were termed by the army is not found, nor do we know who Shadburne reported to after Hampton's departure. Perhaps Shadburne's detachment was designated as "Independent Scouts," but absolutely no hint attesting to their status at this time is found. However, several incidents of significance are found, demonstrating that neither he nor his men had lost any degree of enthusiasm, courage or aggressiveness.

On January 23, Shadburne and his men settled a score with a company of U.S. Colored Troops cavalry carrying a reputation of abusing local citizens. A Richmond newspaper included this account:

> *Captain Shadburne's scouts* [cut] *the Yankee telegraph line about one mile from Cabin Point. The Yankees soon discovered the disconnection, and sent out an operator and an ambulance containing material for repairs, guarded by an escort of thirty-five Negro cavalry....When they came in sight our scouts charged them, killing eleven,...capturing twenty-four horses, the ambulance and material, the operator and driver, and put the rest...to flight.*[190]

Shadburne wrote about those with him in this engagement: "Our number was sixteen, composed of eleven regular scouts, four Confederates I picked up for the occasion, and a man in blue [Yankee deserter] who had come to us by chance."[191] It is apparent that Shadburne and his reduced platoon were still a powerful strike force.

The newspaper article closed, "Since their operations in Grant's rear, Captain Shadburne's scouts have turned over to the government one hundred and twenty horses, eighty mules and some valuable material."[192] Besides the sensational account of the ambush, the article provides a couple of tidbits of interest. First, Shadburne was twice referred to as "Captain," suggesting a change of status, but that was probably a simple mistake. Second, this is the only known attempt by anyone to quantify the Scouts' contributions, but unfortunately, it does not identify the source of the numbers.

The same Richmond newspaper published another article a few days later highlighting another action involving Shadburne—this time with his correct rank—and his Scouts against an enemy attempt to interrupt Confederate activities along the James River. The article reads in part that

> *about two hundred and fifty Yankees, belonging to celebrated Naval Brigade, were defeated and routed by a comparatively small force of Confederate scouts, under command of Sergeant Shadburne, assisted by a party of the independent signal corps....While resting at Burwell's bay, this force was vigorously attacked by the scouts and signal corps men, who eventually succeeded in killing and wounding a number and putting the balance to flight. Sixteen dead bodies were subsequently found....A number of wounded Yankees were carried off by their comrades.*[193]

This remarkable encounter is unusual in several ways. First, it was well outside the normal operational area of Shadburne and his men. Second, this is the only known instance in which they joined with the Signal Corps. Finally, these circumstances point to a directive from a source at, or very near, the top of the Army of Northern Virginia's chain of command, which sent Shadburne's platoon on what must have been considered a "very special" mission. It is comparable to that in which J.E.B. Stuart sent Hampton's Scouts to temporarily unite with Mosby in 1863. The two Scout platoons probably totaled about forty men in this strike, which, unlike the raid with Mosby, was highly successful.

On March 7, Shadburne and fellow Scout James Sloan were captured in a Yankee raid on Fredericksburg. Some sources say they were on furlough there, while others indicate they were on a special mission. Whatever the case, their timing was bad, because a Yankee expedition to Fredericksburg from Fort Monroe arrived on March 5 with gunboats protecting transports carrying infantry and cavalry. The Yankee force took over the city and captured a train, a vast amount of provisions and many wagons with mules. They burned a bridge and a depot and placed captured tobacco on their transports. The next morning, a building-by-building search through the city netted thirteen Confederate soldiers. Among them were Shadburne and Sloan, who were taken after a brief shootout along one of the city streets.

Shadburne and Sloan gave false names to their captors, but Shadburne was quickly identified by documents found on him and recognized "as a notorious guerrilla, and is well known to the Army of the Potomac as a desperado, whose capture has long been desired."[194] In his after-action report, the expedition commander named and praised the three men who captured Shadburne and Sloan, not for bravery in effecting the capture, but for declining to accept Shadburne's offer of $3,000 each if they would allow him and Sloan to go free. Shadburne's offer was almost certainly an empty escape ploy since the report made no mention of any such money found on the prisoners.[195]

Taken first to Fort Monroe, Shadburne and Sloan were sent to a prison barge in the James River near City Point, Grant's headquarters, instead of a prisoner-of-war camp, on March 10. This was a highly unusual move, and the reasons behind it are unknown. Perhaps Grant and his generals wanted to meet Shadburne, by now something of a legend, in person. Perhaps he and Sloan were to be interrogated, tried as spies or outlaws and executed. Whatever the reason, Shadburne delivered another stunning blow and embarrassing moment to the Yankees when he and Sloan escaped before any meetings or trials could take place.

The intrepid pair slipped their shackles one night, commandeered a skiff and made it safely down the James River through the Union flotilla to a site in the proximity of their operational area. Two days later, they encountered another Scout, who rejoiced at seeing them and took them to a camp site for a joyful reunion.[196] This is the last mention of the Scouts in Virginia. Richmond fell shortly afterward, and no Scouts are found on the Appomattox parole records. Shadburne is next found in early April with Wade Hampton in North Carolina.

January–April 1865 (The Carolinas)

T he Scouts who followed Wade Hampton to South Carolina were retained in that capacity. From early February until Joseph Johnston's surrender of his army to General W.T. Sherman in North Carolina two months later, they were constantly in the saddle. Hampton, recently promoted to lieutenant general, had the luxury of having the cavalry of Major General Joseph Wheeler added to his command. Wheeler also provided his extraordinary scouting detachment, Shannon's Scouts, an invaluable asset, taking much of the scouting load off Hampton's reduced platoon.

Sergeant Dick Hogan (Butler's chief scout) wrote that he was tasked by General Hampton to "take [his] party of scouts and locate Sherman's advance, ascertain his movements, and report at the earliest possible moment....I took Shoolbred, Colvin, Dulin, Guffin and Sanders and… Adolphus Kennerly [*sic*]."[197] After riding to a point along the Edisto River some distance from Columbia, they learned of Union activity in the vicinity on the previous day. Hogan and his men dismounted, proceeded on foot some distance and found the main body of the enemy. After a detailed reconnaissance and gathering a great deal of information from local citizens over a period of two days, Hogan's party departed the area with intentions of reporting that Sherman was likely destined for Columbia rather than Charleston. But before reaching their horses, they interrupted three of Sherman's bummers in the act of robbing a lady in her house. After Hogan and Shoolbred disarmed the culprits, Hogan took one of the Yankee

Wartime sketch of Columbia being burned by Sherman. *Library of Congress.*

horses, intending to ride alone and quickly inform Hampton of what had been learned. His companions, not yet close to their horses, were to follow. Unfortunately, before going far, Hogan inadvertently rode into the midst of a Union regiment and was captured.[198]

Columbia fell to Sherman's army on February 17, after the withdrawal of Confederate forces, and was set ablaze by the Yankee invaders that night. A day or two later, Hampton called for Scout John Colvin, who later recounted the essence of that summons: "General Hampton selected me to go around Sherman's army near Columbia to ascertain if the buildings had been burned by the enemy. General Hampton gave me and my detail breakfast from his own table the morning we started for the city."[199]

The balance of February was spent in a slow withdrawal of Confederate forces across South Carolina. While General Joseph Johnston was trying desperately to gather sufficient forces to meet Sherman's sixty-thousand-man army, Hampton's Scouts rode furiously to keep a close watch on Union movements. In this dark period, they provided distinguished service through extraordinary efforts to keep their generals informed and to hurt their foe when the opportunities arose.

On February 23, Major General Matthew Butler and part of his cavalry were met not far from Florence, South Carolina, by Private James Dulin, one of Hampton's most aggressive Scouts. Dulin reported that "about 200 Yankee infantry foragers were engaged in pillaging Mr. Cantey's house and outbuildings preparatory to applying the torch."[200] He also advised the Yankees had stacked arms, meaning they would be highly vulnerable. Butler immediately dispatched a portion of his command, the Fourth South Carolina under Colonel Zimmerman Davis, to go with Dulin and "to bag the last one."[201]

The Confederate cavalry arrived at the nearby farm undetected, formed a line and charged on the enemy. One witness remembered the attack: "Dulin, like a tiger on his prey, horse and rider sprang among them and as rapidly as you could fire a 'right or left' at partridges, two bummers lay dead (he had a knack of killing, not wounding). He scored a third just afterwards and more for aught I know."[202]

Colonel Davis wrote, "It was but the work of a few moments…about two hundred prisoners and nineteen splendid army wagons, each drawn by six fine mules clad in such harness as our Confederate teamsters had not seen for many a day."[203] He added, "Jim Dulin was severely wounded in the thigh and the best we could do for him was to put him in a little hut near the river in Darlington County."[204]

Dulin was not left there long, for (presumably) General Butler arranged for him to be carried via a wagon to Cheraw. There he was tended to by an old friend and fellow Scout, Newt Fowles, who had recently bought his way out of a Union prisoner-of-war camp. Fowles obtained a buggy and mule, arranged the buggy to comfortably accommodate Dulin's leg and drove him to Greensboro, North Carolina, a trip of over one hundred miles. There, he placed Dulin on a train that would carry him back to his beloved Virginia.[205] The war was over for James Dulin.

Hampton's Scouts, in conjunction with Shannon's Scouts and other cavalry elements, kept tabs on Sherman's cavalry, led by General Judson Kilpatrick. The timely, accurate and detailed reports led to the Battle of Monroe's Crossroads on March 10, in which Kilpatrick's command was surprised, mauled and nearly destroyed by Confederate cavalry. Kilpatrick, though ultimately victorious, was nearly captured and exceedingly embarrassed.

Very early the next day, Wade Hampton and a handful of men battled an advance force of Union cavalry in the middle of Fayetteville, North Carolina. This action, though small in scale, is especially notable for the personal involvement of Hampton. It began when Private Hugh Scott rushed to Hampton, still at breakfast in a hotel, with news that Yankee cavalry was in town. Hampton recalled, "One of my scouts, a beardless

Wartime sketch of Union bummers from General W.T. Sherman's army. *Library of Congress.*

boy, Scott by name,…said, 'General, there are not over a hundred Yankees here. Give me five or six men and I will whip them out of town.' That boy so inspired me, that I said, 'You scouts, follow me.'"[206] Hampton had three couriers from the Fourth South Carolina, another man from Wheeler's command and Hugh Scott.[207]

Having mounted their horses, they soon encountered an enemy platoon, which opened fire on them. Hampton, without hesitation, ordered his men to charge, and the fight was on. Scott wrote, "We charged right up to them and shoved our pistols right in their faces and got them started on the run.…I looked and saw some behind us."[208] A second platoon was forming for attack, but Hampton and his stalwart men opened fire on them as they came into the open. The action ended abruptly when the surviving Yanks fled the city with Hampton and his men right behind them.

With the threat vanquished, Hampton and his little band of cavalrymen took stock of what had transpired in the space of just a few minutes. Thirteen Yankees had been killed, and among the dozen captured were the chief scouts for both Sherman's Seventeenth Army Corps and the Army of the Tennessee. From them, Hampton and his little band learned the Union force had totaled sixty-eight men. Not a single Confederate was harmed in this engagement, thus adding yet another page to the Iron

Scouts' legacy.[209] Hampton is said to have personally killed two, possibly more, Yankees that day.[210]

Continual patrolling by all of Hampton's cavalry resulted in detailed information, allowing Generals Hampton and Joseph Johnston to set the stage for the Battle of Bentonville. There, the opposing armies fought for three days, and Johnston's little army came close to victory. In the end, the Confederate forces were forced to retreat, but they did so knowing they had bloodied Sherman's nose.

A few days after the battle, Scouts Hugh Scott, N.B. Eison and several others hit a Union camp near Snow Hill, North Carolina, at night and took nineteen horses. In this same patrol, they captured another fifty-six. Scott wrote, "Generals Hampton and Butler…were delighted at the results of our trip, for in those dark days seventy-five horses was no mean gift to the cavalrymen."[211]

The final reference to Hampton's Scouts in the *Official Records* is found in a March 23 message from Hampton to General Johnston. It reads, in part, "General: I forward a dispatch from Ashby, one of my best scouts. He is very accurate in his information."[212]

After Bentonville, probably in early April following the fall of Richmond, Sergeant George Shadburne showed up at Hampton's headquarters. Shortly afterward, Hampton assigned him the boldest and most difficult mission likely given during the war: Hampton wanted Shadburne to go after General W.T. Sherman, as Hampton had learned he was in a specific house in Goldsboro. The essence of Hampton's instructions was that Shadburne was to capture Sherman or kill him.[213]

Shadburne took thirty men for the mission, but bad weather, swollen rivers and lots of Yankee cavalry blocked his every move. By the time he reached Goldsboro, Sherman had moved on. In the end, Shadburne and his daring party left their mark well behind Sherman's front by capturing one hundred wagons and four hundred mules. The small party could bring just eighteen wagons and one hundred mules to Confederate lines.[214]

Shortly afterward, Joseph Johnston surrendered his army to Sherman at Bennett Place near Durham, North Carolina. Hampton's Scouts, like the rest of the Confederate army, disbanded and went home. No Scout took parole then, but several did accept it after returning home. Few are found to have later taken the hated Oath of Allegiance.

A number of Scouts still languished in Union prisoner-of-war camps after April, but all were released by the end of June. Two, however, were unable to return home after receiving parole because they were hospitalized at

Point Lookout. Solomon Legare and Wallace Miller, captured the previous November, were admitted to the hospital with chronic diarrhea on July 2. Miller recovered sufficiently to care for and encourage his friend. Sadly, poor Legare succumbed to the ravages of his sickness on July 22, and several days later, Wallace Miller departed the hospital alone to begin his journey home.[215]

EPILOGUE

I n 1868, Wallace Miller returned to Point Lookout, claimed the remains of Solomon Legare and brought them to Legare's family in Charleston, South Carolina, for reburial. This act of brotherly love and compassion, three years after Appomattox, was the final mission for Hampton's Scouts.[216]

Any summary of their service would almost certainly testify that they surpassed the hopes and expectations of their creators, Generals Robert E. Lee, J.E.B. Stuart and Wade Hampton. Historians generally credit the Scouts with detecting each of Grant's moves below Petersburg in 1864, with the possible exception of the December 1 Stoney Creek Depot cavalry raid. One source asserts, "It is hard to place the proper estimate upon the great work that the scouts accomplished for the Confederate government. They kept General Lee better posted as to the movements of the Yankee army than a great many of the Union generals knew themselves."[217] That same source declared, "All of Butler's scouts [and, by extension, those of Hampton] deserved promotion, but they could not be spared from that very dangerous and peculiar duty which required nerve and intelligence as but few men possessed."[218]

A theme popular among some historians and authors is that the Scouts routinely wore captured Union uniforms. However, not a single incident is found in which a captured Scout was wearing one. That they wore captured Union coats in the winter is certainly documented, but not one of the twenty-nine Scouts captured was treated as a spy, which would certainly have been the case had any been wearing a complete Union uniform. Surprisingly, too, there are no reports of Scouts being abused after capture despite the heavy-handed orders and threats from Union commanders regarding "bushwhackers and guerrillas."

Sergeants Bill Mickler and George Shadburne were simply outstanding in their individual tenures as commander of Hampton's Scouts. Shadburne is widely known to scholars because of his role in the Great Beefsteak Raid and his postwar writings. Mickler, who did not write of his wartime experiences, is unfairly overshadowed and overlooked. Both were fortunate to be so ably supported by a roster filled with courageous, daring and intelligent young men who carried out incredible feats.

Of the fifty-six Scouts for whom ages are known, twenty-two were under the age of twenty at the outbreak of the war. Two of these, John Chapman and Lem Guffin, were fifteen years old and two others just sixteen. Just six were above age twenty-five, and two of those, James McCalla and Bernard King, were above the age of thirty.

A remarkable resemblance exists in the variety of missions carried out by Hampton's Scouts and U.S. reconnaissance units in the Vietnam War. The Scouts' methods of operation were, in a large degree, unknowingly mirrored over one hundred years later by marine recon teams, army LRRPs and special forces. All these men, whether from the 1860s or the late twentieth century, shared the same inherent attributes of boldness, intelligence and self-discipline when in the field with their lives in constant peril. The twenty-first-century special-operations commands can look to these predecessors not only with pride but also for inspiration.

ANNOTATED ROSTER
OF HAMPTON'S SCOUTS

The paucity of detail within the Compiled Service Records for most of these men is apparent. It is impossible to know a man's wartime service based solely on them but, in many instances, they provide information pertinent to this study. Service records for some, such as E. Prioleau Henderson, were huge disappointments. Not a single mention of Henderson's scouting is within his record, yet his book *Autobiography of Arab* provides extensive detail of his approximate fourteen months in Hampton's Scouts. Service records for several others simply do not exist at all.

This annotated roster is composed of information gathered from a variety of sources. Compiled Service Records, family histories, newspaper accounts, obituaries, census records, findagrave.com, postwar books and magazine articles were utilized. Especially important were the accounts written by the Scouts themselves. The authors took great pains to identify and share credit with those riding beside them in a fight or memorable scouting mission. Without these accounts, some men would not have their scouting recorded at all.

A large number of men, some of whom were prominent Scouts, seemingly just disappeared after the war. Of the sixty-four who survived the war, only forty-five were found in postwar records. Their focus, having shifted from wartime duties in 1865, was directed to making a living and providing for growing families. This they accomplished in a highly credible manner. They became successful farmers, merchants, businessmen and attorneys. Additionally, there were three physicians, two prominent newspapermen, a judge, a justice of the peace, a police chief and an artist. Six are known to have lived beyond 1920, and the last, J.S. Harris, eventually "crossed the river" in 1936.

ADAMS, JOEL R. | Private, Company K, Fourth South Carolina Cavalry
Born about 1844 in Richland County, South Carolina, Joel R. Adams was the son of a planter. Originally entered military service with the Sixth South Carolina Infantry in March 1862 but medically discharged in May 1862 after a bout with typhoid fever. Enlisted in Fourth South Carolina Cavalry on January 1, 1863, at Pocotaligo, South Carolina. Appointed daily regimental bugler. Mentioned as late war Scout in postwar articles by other Scouts. Adams worked as a farmer after the war and died in 1914 in Richland County, South Carolina.

ASHBY, WALTER S. | Private, Company B, Jeff Davis Legion
Born about 1834 in Virginia, the 1850 census shows Ashby living in Marengo, Alabama. He enlisted on December 9, 1862, in Culpepper County, Virginia. Admitted to hospital in Charlottesville, Virginia, on June 29, 1863, and placed on forty-day wounded furlough on July 1, 1863, he was recommended for the captaincy of his company in 1864. A letter sent to President Jefferson Davis attesting to his qualifications is in his service record with his scouting experience noted. He was a highly respected Scout who led numerous scouting parties in providing meritorious service. Prior to his scouting, Ashby served with the Fourteenth Mississippi Infantry dating to May 1861 as a second lieutenant. Captured at Fort Donelson in February 1862 and held as prisoner of war at Johnson's Island, Ashby resigned his commission in September 1862.

BARNWELL, WOODWARD | Sergeant, Company H, Second South Carolina Cavalry
Born about 1838 in South Carolina, Barnwell enlisted on July 17, 1861, in Columbia, South Carolina. Nothing pertaining to his service as a scout for Hampton is in his records, but he is frequently mentioned in accounts from other Scouts. Following the return of his regiment to South Carolina in early 1864, several references attesting to his scouting duties for the Department of South Carolina, George and Florida are noted, including a letter commending his scouting of Port Royal. After the war, Barnwell farmed in Georgia and Florida before dying in 1927 in Fernandina, Florida. He is buried in Savannah, Georgia.

BECK, JOSIAH | Corporal, Company B, Second South Carolina Cavalry
Born about 1844 in Colleton County, South Carolina, Beck enlisted at
Grahamsville, South Carolina, on June 19, 1861. Captured on April 13,
1863, near Cedar Run, Virginia (Brentsville), he was sent to Old Capitol
Prison, Washington, D.C. Beck claimed to have risen to the rank of sergeant
and worked as a merchant and farmer after the war and before his death in
1904 in Beaufort, South Carolina.

BLACK, FRANKLIN H. "GUS" | Private, Company B, Jeff Davis Legion
Black enlisted originally at Carolton, Alabama, on June 11, 1861, in
Company C, Eleventh Alabama Infantry, but transferred to the Legion
in early 1863. Company muster roll for the period of May 1 through
August 1863 reports him on detached duty as division scout. He was in
a Richmond hospital from October 6, 1863, through February 1864 and
on light duty as guard at Howards' Grove Hospital in Richmond at least
through May 1864. Black was included in the surrender at Citronelle,
Alabama, by General Taylor on May 4, 1865. Paroled May 20, 1865.

BOLICK, WILLIAM A. | Private, Company K, First South Carolina Cavalry
Bolick was born around 1844 in Catawba, North Carolina, but lived
in Chester, South Carolina, prior to the war. The son of a blacksmith,
he enlisted on July 12, 1862, after serving a one-year enlistment in First
South Carolina Infantry (Butler's). Company muster rolls for September
through December 1863 show him absent scouting. The roll for January
and February 1864 simply states, "Killed in action." He died in scouting
duties at Brentsville, Virginia, on February 14, 1864, and was buried by
Hampton's Scouts at Arrington's Crossroads (now David's Crossroads),
which later was absorbed by Quantico Marine Corps base.

BRADLEY, JOHN A. | Private, Company A, Second South Carolina Cavalry
Bradley, born about 1843 in Chester, South Carolina, withdrew from the
South Carolina Military Academy (The Citadel) after his second year
and enlisted on June 21, 1861. He was detached as a scout from late 1863
through early 1864. A transfer to the First South Carolina Artillery was
approved in late 1864, but no record is found showing it taking place.
An attorney and judge after the war, Bradley died in Volusia County,
Florida, in 1910.

BRENT, JAMES H. | Sergeant, Company B, Cobb's Legion
Brent enlisted on August 14, 1861, in Atlanta, Georgia. Promoted several times, he reached the rank of third sergeant in late 1862. Detailed as sergeant of Colonel Brooks' couriers on April 1, 1863, and as a scout on November 13, 1863, he was captured on March 2, 1864, in Stafford County, Virginia (Morrisville). Brent was received at Old Capitol Prison in Washington, D.C., on March 10, 1864, admitted to the hospital on March 22,1864, and discharged on April 6, 1864. He was transferred to Fort Delaware, Delaware, on June 17, 1864.

BUTLER, THOMAS L. | Sergeant, Company I, Second South Carolina Cavalry
Born in 1841, Butler was killed in action at Gettysburg on July 3, 1863. Per his obituary, he declined a lieutenancy. His body was exhumed from Gettysburg and reburied in Greenville, South Carolina, in 1865. He was the younger brother of Major General M.C. Butler.

CARROLL, S.L. | Sergeant, Company D, Jeff Davis Legion
Born about 1836 in South Carolina, Carroll was living in Marengo, Alabama, in 1860. Census records give his first name as Sylvanus. He enlisted on August 10, 1861, in Montgomery, Alabama, and was named color sergeant of the Legion in June 1862. Detached as a scout on January 10, 1864, he was captured on March 2, 1864, near Morrisville, Virginia. Carroll was transferred to Fort Delaware on June 17, 1864, and released on June 11, 1865. He farmed after the war and died in Cabarrus County, North Carolina, in 1912.

CHAPMAN, JOHN L. | Private, Company A, Jeff Davis Legion
Born in 1846 in Newberry, South Carolina, Chapman was living in Mississippi in 1860. He enlisted on June 22, 1861, in Ashland, Virginia. Records show him detached as a scout from January 11, 1864, through September 30, 1864, except for a furlough of indulgence in April.

CLOYD, T. SHELBY | Private, Company A, Jeff Davis Legion
Born about 1841 in Alabama, Cloyd transferred to the Jeff Davis Legion in January 1863 from the Seventh South Carolina Infantry. Captured while scouting on December 13, 1863, he was exchanged on November 1, 1864. After the war, he was employed as a clerk in Alabama; he died sometime after 1870.

COLVIN, JOHN C. | Private, regiment unidentified
Colvin, a young Virginian, served in Hampton's Scouts, but no service records are found. He is mentioned in several accounts by other Scouts and had a couple of postwar articles on his service. His obituary references his service and states he was buried in his Confederate uniform. Born in 1845 in Prince William County, Virginia, Colvin, who farmed after the war, died there in 1921.

CRAFTON, GEORGE M. | Private, Company I, Second South Carolina Cavalry
Born about 1839, Crafton studied at the University of Virginia. He enlisted on October 8, 1861, and company muster rolls for May and June 1863 and July and August 1863 list him as "absent on detached service." Subsequent musters through December 1864 show him "present." He died in Edgefield County, South Carolina, in 1877.

DULIN, JAMES R. | Private, Company A, Second South Carolina Cavalry
Born about 1844 in Fauquier County, Virginia, Dulin enlisted on March 14, 1862. He was captured on March 28, 1863, and exchanged shortly afterward. Company muster rolls for May and June 1863 and July and August 1863 show him "On detached service-Scout for Gen'l Stuart." On September 22, 1863, Dulin was again captured, this time near Madison Court House, Virginia (Catlett's Station), and sent to Old Capitol Prison in Washington, D.C., prior to being transferred to Point Lookout, Maryland. Available records show he was held there several months (accounts state that he bought his way out of prison) and is shown as being "a scout for Major General Hampton since April 1, 1864" on company muster rolls for May and June 1864 and July–August 1864. Wounded in February 1865, Dulin returned to his Virginia home. He lost four, or perhaps five, brothers in the war (Billy, John, Melvin, Edward and Lemuel). James Dulin farmed after the war and died in Platte County, Missouri, in 1875.

EISON, NAPOLEON BONAPARTE | Private, Company K, Fifth South Carolina Cavalry
Born in Colleton County, South Carolina, in 1838, Eison enlisted in Confederate service in December 1861. He served in the Sixth South Carolina Infantry (six-month regiment), Eighteenth South Carolina Infantry (as a first lieutenant) and Sixth South Carolina Cavalry (Company F, "Cadet Rangers") before transferring to the Fifth South Carolina Cavalry. A salesman and farmer after the war, Eison was active in the United Confederate

Veterans organization before his death in Union County, South Carolina, in 1919. He was probably an occasional member of Hampton's Scouts.

ELLIOTT, JOHN S. | Private, Company D, Jeff Davis Legion
Elliott enlisted at age twenty-two on August 10, 1861, in Montgomery, Alabama. Detached as a scout on January 10, 1864, he served in that capacity for much, if not all, of 1864.

FOWLES, JOHN NEWTON | Private, Company I, Second South Carolina Cavalry
Born about 1841 in Walterboro, South Carolina, Fowles enlisted on June 14, 1861. Records for May through December 1863 list him as "absent on detached service." He was captured December 14, 1863, at Rappahannock, Virginia, and remained a prisoner until late 1864, when he bought his way out of the prisoner-of-war camp. Few details of his capture and experience are available. Last records show that he left for South Carolina on December 22, 1864, to procure a horse. He died in Columbia, South Carolina, in 1913, and was buried in Newberry. Fowles's obituary noted that he was a well-known lumber dealer, farmer and veteran.

GUFFIN, JAMES T. | Private, Company G, Second South Carolina Cavalry
Guffin was born around 1836 in Abbeville, South Carolina. He enlisted on April 10, 1862, at the Peninsula, Virginia. There are multiple references to his scouting in 1863 and 1864. Captured on March 20, 1863, near Elk Run in Prince William County, Virginia, he was sent to Old Capitol Prison in Washington, D.C. A letter from his regimental adjutant states he served as a scout for Hampton from August 23, 1863, until recalled to his regiment on January 18, 1864. Documents also show that he took a twenty-one-day furlough on February 22, 1864, and returned to Virginia in March 1864 "by order of General Hampton." On May 31, 1864, he was admitted to Jackson Hospital in Richmond with a gunshot wound to his right shoulder and furloughed for thirty days on June 5, 1864. All entries after this date reflect that he was still scouting. He and his brothers were known as Jim, Lem and Pem. Jim died in Lee County, Texas, in 1918.

GUFFIN, LAWRENCE PEMBERTON | Company and Regiment unknown
Guffin was born in 1846 in Abbeville, South Carolina. There are no official records attesting to his military service, but he is mentioned in accounts by other Scouts and certainly followed his two brothers with Wade Hampton to Virginia in the spring of 1864. Pem died in South Carolina in 1880.

GUFFIN, LEMUEL L. | Company and Regiment unidentified
Guffin was born in 1844 in Abbeville, South Carolina. He was medically discharged on October 23, 1862, from the Second South Carolina Rifles. No records have been found showing later service, but he accompanied his brothers to Virginia in 1864 to serve as a scout and guide at the request of Wade Hampton. Lem died in Beaufort, South Carolina, in 1889.

HANLEY, GEORGE J. | Private, Company H, First North Carolina Cavalry
Born about 1843 in Chatham County, North Carolina, Hanley enlisted in Charles City, Virginia, in July 7, 1862. Detailed as a scout in November 1862, he was reported as AWOL from late 1863 until his return in February 1864 and held in Castle Thunder, Richmond, under suspicion of being a deserter and a Federal spy. Hanley was released and returned to his command in February 1865.

HARRIS, JULIUS SHAKESPEARE | Private, Company F, First North Carolina Cavalry
Harris was born in Cabarrus County in 1845, enlisted in Mecklenberg County, North Carolina, on February 15, 1863, and was officially detached as a scout in March–April 1864. Captured near Petersburg on November 7, 1864, and held at Point Lookout, Maryland, he was considered exchanged on March 14, 1865, but not released until June 27, 1865. Harris served as commander of a North Carolina UCV division. The successful postwar farmer, landlord and cotton mill investor died in Cabarrus County, North Carolina, in 1936.

HARRISON, J.J. | Sergeant, Company D, Jeff Davis Legion
Born in 1839, Harrison enlisted on August 10, 1861, in Montgomery, Alabama. Admitted to Chimborazo Hospital on July 16, 1863, with a shell wound in right shoulder, he returned to duty on January 23, 1864, and was detached as a scout shortly afterward. Harrison was captured on March 1, 1864, near Fairfax, Virginia, and taken to Old Capitol Prison, Washington, D.C., from which he escaped at 3:00 a.m. on August 10, 1864.

HASKELL, WILLIAM E. | Sergeant, Company H, Second South Carolina Cavalry
Haskell enlisted on July 17, 1861, was captured at Kelly's Ford, Virginia, on March 17, 1863, and then exchanged at City Point, Virginia, less than two weeks later on March 29, 1863.

HENAGAN, A. BERNARD | Private, Second South Carolina Cavalry
Henagan is mentioned prominently in accounts written by other Scouts. Prioleau Henderson wrote that Henagan was born about 1836, studied law and frequently defended soldiers in courts-martial. His service record shows substantial scouting. Supposedly, he led an independent squad of Scouts and was promoted to the rank of captain. Captured in March 1864 and held as a prisoner until after war's end, Henagan died sometime in the 1880s, according to Henderson.

HENDERSON, E. PRIOLEAU | Sergeant, Company B, Second South Carolina Cavalry
Born in 1842 in Colleton County, South Carolina, Henderson attended Wofford College and enlisted on June 19, 1861, in Grahamsville, South Carolina. There is no mention at all of scouting in his service records. He was paroled at Augusta, Georgia, on May 23, 1865. He is the author of *Autobiography of Arab*, in which he detailed his wartime service of about fourteen months as a member of Hampton's Scouts. Henderson lived and worked in Savannah, Georgia, before his death in Walterboro, South Carolina, in 1910.

HODGES, WILLIAM H. | Sergeant, Company D, Jeff Davis Legion
Born about 1839, Hodges enlisted on August 10, 1861, in Montgomery, Alabama. Promoted to first sergeant on June 1, 1863, he was detached as a scout on January 10, 1864, but reduced in rank to private for accepting the scouting appointment. Hodges was wounded on June 20, 1864.

HOGAN, J. DICKERSON | Sergeant, Company I, Second South Carolina Cavalry
Born in 1838 in Fairfield County, South Carolina, Hogan enlisted on June 14, 1861, in Columbia, South Carolina. Records show he was officially detached as a scout on June 1, 1863, and served in that capacity until captured in February 1865. Indications are that he was considered second in command of the Scouts under both Mickler and Shadburne. Hogan moved to Pope County, Arkansas, in the 1880s and was a successful farmer until his death in 1922. He served as a justice of the peace and a member of the Arkansas legislature.

HORD, WILLIAM HENRY | Private, Company D, Jeff Davis Legion
Hord enlisted on June 29, 1861, in Sumter, Alabama. He was present or accounted for on all muster rolls through late 1864. Records show he was detached as a scout on February 11, 1864, and remained in that capacity at least into November.

HUTCHINSON, PHILLIP H. | Private, Company K, Fourth South Carolina Cavalry
Hutchinson enlisted on July 10, 1862, was wounded in action on May 28, 1864, and detached as a scout on September 30, 1864. Prior to his scouting, he served with the First South Carolina Cavalry (militia) as a private and with the Hampton Legion artillery battalion as a second lieutenant.

JOHNSON, R. CECIL | Private, Company K, Second South Carolina Cavalry
Johnson was killed in action on June 21, 1863, at Upperville, Virginia, and buried there. His father was chaplain of the First South Carolina Cavalry. He enlisted on May 22, 1861, in the Eighth Georgia Infantry but transferred to Hampton's Legion on September 12, 1861.

KENNEDY, WILLIAM ADOLPHUS | Private, Company H, Second South Carolina Cavalry
Detailed as a scout for Hampton on May 1, 1864, Kennedy was captured on October 11, 1864, the same day Scout W.W. Russell was captured, on Jerusalem Plank Road near Petersburg, Virginia, and sent to Point Lookout. The following note was sent with him: "[He is a] scout and has been lurking around our rear. Should be held until such time as that information he may be possessed of will do no injury to our army." Considered exchanged on February 13, 1865, Kennedy was paroled five days later and received in Richmond on March 28, 1865.

KING, THOMAS BERNARD | Private, Company I, Second South Carolina Cavalry
Born 1830 in the District of Columbia, King enlisted on June 28, 1863, and may have had prior service. Records attest that he was detached as a scout as early as March 1, 1864. An attorney after the war, he died in Charleston, South Carolina, about 1878.

KNAPP, AARON CHAMPION | Sergeant, Company F, Jeff Davis Legion
Born in 1841 in Chatham County, Georgia, Knapp's service records confirm he was one of Hampton's Scouts from January 7, 1864, until the end of March 1864. His company was originally Company E, Sixth Virginia Cavalry, but it was transferred to the Jeff Davis Legion in late 1861. He worked as a bookkeeper and railroad clerk in Savannah, Georgia, after the war and died in 1897.

LATHAM, DANIEL F. | Sergeant, Company D, Jeff Davis Legion
Latham enlisted at age twenty-four on August 10, 1861, in Montgomery, Alabama. Detached as a Scout on January 10, 1864, he was captured on March 31, 1864, at Falmouth, Virginia, received at Old Capitol Prison in Washington, D.C., on April 8, 1864, and was held two months before being delivered to Fort Delaware on June 17, 1864. Latham was released on June 11, 1865.

LEGARE, SOLOMON E. | Private, Company F, Sixth South Carolina Cavalry
Born about 1840 in Charleston, South Carolina, Legare was the son of a planter. He enlisted on April 15, 1861, and was detailed as a Scout on September 28, 1864. Legare was captured on November 7, 1864, near Petersburg and sent to Washington, D.C., four days later. He was considered exchanged on March 14, 1865, at Point Lookout but not released until June 28, 1865. Unable to travel, he was hospitalized at Point Lookout on July 2, 1865, where he died on July 22, 1865. In 1868, W.W. Miller, a fellow Scout, returned to Point Lookout, recovered Legare's remains and brought them to Legare's family in Charleston. This is considered to have been the last mission of Hampton's Scouts.

LIDE, LEIGHTON W. | Private, Company A, Second South Carolina Cavalry
Born in 1838, in Darlington County, South Carolina, Lide was the son of a planter. He attended Furman University and the University of Virginia and was in medical school in New York when the war began. Lide enlisted on September 8, 1861, and transferred to the Sixth South Carolina Cavalry on July 10, 1863. His service record is sparse, but there is an application for a commission in the First South Carolina Artillery in September 1863 that was denied for lack of vacancy. One letter of recommendation with his application refers to others who would attest to "his worth as a man, his gallantry and fidelity as a soldier." After the war, Lide was a farmer and died in Darlington County in 1910.

LOGAN, ROSWELL F. | Private, Company A, Second South Carolina Cavalry
Born in Charleston, South Carolina, in 1836, Logan was the son of an English librarian. He enlisted on June 26, 1861, and was present or accounted for subsequent muster rolls. There is no mention of scouting within his records, but accounts from other Scouts attest to his scouting, probably as an occasional Scout. An attorney after the war, Logan also served as the night editor of Charleston's *News & Courier* newspaper. He died in 1906.

McCALLA, JAMES D. | Sergeant, Company H, First South Carolina Cavalry
Born about 1829 in Chester County, South Carolina, McCalla worked as a mechanic/machinist until the start of the war. He enlisted on March 14, 1862, in Rock Hill, South Carolina, and was detached as a scout for General Hampton on April 22, 1864. McCalla was killed on September 16, 1864, in the Great Beefsteak Raid and is probably one of the thirty thousand unidentified Confederate soldiers buried at Blandford Cemetery in Petersburg, Virginia. He saw prior service as an artificer in the First South Carolina Artillery and was reduced in ranks to private when he volunteered to return to Virginia as a scout for Hampton in 1864.

McCLURE, F.M. | Private, Company H, Sixth South Carolina Cavalry
McClure's service record is sparse, with no mention of scouting. Accounts from other Scouts confirm he served in a scouting role probably on an occasional basis. Shadburne mentioned McClure's presence in an ambush on January 23, 1865, as his regiment was returning to South Carolina. This indicates McClure might have remained in Virginia to scout for Shadburne.

McCOY, A.J. | Private, Company E, Jeff Davis Legion
Born about 1839, McCoy was the son of a farmer. He enlisted on July 18, 1861, in Marengo, Alabama, and was captured while scouting near Fairfax, Virginia, on March 3, 1864. He was sent to Fort Delaware on September 19, 1864, and released on June 11, 1865. McCoy died in Tennessee sometime after 1891.

McILWAYNE, JOHN H. | Private, Company A, Jeff Davis Legion
Born about 1836 in Pennsylvania but living in Natchez, Mississippi, in 1860, McIlwayne enlisted on May 18, 1861, in Natchez. His service record is sparse, with no mention of scouting, but accounts of other Scouts confirm his role as a Scout. He was captured in March 1864 and exchanged the following September.

MERCHANT, RUFUS B. | Private, Company A, Cobb's Legion
Born about 1838 in Virginia, Merchant was living in Augusta, Georgia, at the time of his enlistment in August 1861. Detailed as a scout on September 1, 1863, he is thought to have served in that capacity until the end of the war. Paroled on May 26, 1865, in Augusta, after the war, Merchant worked as a printer, bookseller, editor and newspaper owner. He died in the District of Columbia in 1905 and is buried in Fredericksburg, Virginia.

MICKLER, HUGER | Hampton Legion Cavalry
Born about 1834 in Georgia, Mickler grew up in Beaufort County, South Carolina, the son of a blacksmith. Before the war, he worked as a wheelwright. Corporal Mickler was the older brother of William A. Mickler, and he was killed in action in the spring of 1863 in Prince William County, Virginia, and buried near Dale City. He transferred from the Eighth Georgia Infantry to the Hampton Legion Cavalry along with Cecil Johnson.

MICKLER, WILLIAM A. | First Lieutenant, Company B, Second South Carolina Cavalry
Born about 1840, Mickler enlisted on June 19, 1861, in Grahamsville, South Carolina. No mention of his scouting is found in his records except for the company muster roll for September and October 1863, which simply states, "Absent, Scouting." He served as the first commander of Hampton's Scouts, and the muster roll for January and February 1864 states that he was "absent, wounded since 16 Dec last near Brentsville, VA." Mickler was promoted from sergeant to lieutenant on October 15, 1863, under the Valor and Skill Act of 1862. He is the younger brother of Huger Mickler. A postwar farmer, county commissioner and sergeant-at-arms of the Florida Senate, Mickler died in St. Augustine, Florida, in 1917.

MILLER, SIMEON E. | Private, Company K, Second South Carolina Cavalry
Born about 1838 in South Carolina, Miller was the son of a planter. He attended Furman University prior to the war and enlisted on June 1, 1861, in Greenville, South Carolina. Wounded and captured at Warrenton Junction, Virginia, on May 3, 1863, he was committed to Old Capitol Prison, Washington, D.C., on May 21, 1863, but exchanged the following month. He farmed in Augusta County, Virginia, for a time and later was a farmer and insurance salesman in Greenwood, South Carolina. Miller died in 1910.

MILLER, WILLIAM WALLACE | Private, Company C, First South Carolina Cavalry
Born in 1843 in Aiken, South Carolina, Miller was the son of a planter. He enlisted on September 18, 1861, in Hamburg, South Carolina, and the muster roll for March–April 1863 shows him on detached service. Several references show him detached as a scout for Hampton in Virginia as of April 15, 1864. Captured below Petersburg on November 15, 1864, and sent to Point Lookout, Maryland, Miller was released on June 29, 1865, but admitted to the prison hospital shortly afterward for chronic diarrhea. He spent several weeks in the hospital before returning home. (See Solomon Legare's entry.) A farmer after the war, he died in Aiken in 1910.

MORROW, WILLIAM B. | Private, Company G, Second South Carolina Cavalry
Born about 1838, Morrow enlisted on April 10, 1862, at Peninsula, Virginia. Wounded and captured on July 19, 1863, at Accotink, Virginia, he was treated at Second Division General Hospital, in Alexandria, Virginia for a flesh wound to the left leg on July 21, 1863. Morrow was transferred to Lincoln General Hospital in Washington on August 4, 1863, and sent to Baltimore on August 22, 1863, paroled at Baltimore and delivered at City Point on August 24, 1863. He was detached as a scout for Hampton in early 1864 and returned to Virginia. His capture at Accotink, just outside Alexandria, is puzzling, for he was about one hundred miles away from Hampton's brigade, which was still near Falling Waters along the Potomac River. It is likely he was acting as a courier between Stuart and Confederate agents near Washington, D.C.

NIBLET, JAMES | Company and Regiment unidentified.
No wartime service or postwar records are found, but he is mentioned by Hugh Scott as being one of Hampton's Scouts.

PARKS, WILLIAM P. | Private, Company A, First North Carolina Cavalry.
Parks enlisted at age eighteen on June 8, 1861, and served initially as a musician. Company muster rolls show him detached as a scout for much of 1863 and 1864. After the war, he became a physician, just like his father. Parks died in Iredell, North Carolina, in 1918.

PIERCE, JOHN H. | Sergeant, Company K, First South Carolina Cavalry
Born in 1842, Pierce enlisted on March 12, 1862, in Company C at Wadmalaw Island, South Carolina, and transferred to Company K on June 27, 1862. He was present or accounted for on subsequent company muster rolls until September–October 1863, when shown as "on detached service by order of Lt. Col. Twiggs." The November–December 1863 roll lists him as "on Scout over Rappahannock since December 3, 1863." Prisoner-of-war records show he was captured near Morrisville, Virginia, on March 1, 1864, and committed to Old Capitol Prison in Washington, D.C. He was transferred to the prison hospital on March 24 for a month, delivered to Fort Delaware on June 17, 1864, and released on June 10, 1865. Pierce died in 1913 near Augusta, Georgia, and wrote several accounts of his wartime experiences.

RIFE, WILLIAM W. | Private, Company A, Jeff Davis Legion
Rife was born about 1839 in Washington County, Mississippi, to a well-to-do family and was working as a deputy recorder at the beginning of the war. He attended Centenary College of Louisiana and enlisted on April 13, 1861, in Jackson, Mississippi. Detached as a scout in mid-1864, Rife became a successful postwar planter and died in Bolivar, Mississippi, in 1905.

RUSSELL, WILLIAM WALKER | Private, Company F, First South Carolina Cavalry
An eighteen-year-old student, Russell enlisted in December 1861 in Pickens County, South Carolina. Records indicate he was on detached service with the Signal Corps from late 1862 through the middle of 1863. The September–October 1863 muster roll lists him as "absent, on scout with permission." He was detached from his command on March 25, 1864, and returned to Virginia with Hampton. Russell was captured on October 11, 1864, at Proctors Crossroads with Scout W.A. Kennedy and sent to City Point with the notation "[He is a] Scout and has been hovering around our rear. Should be held until such time as that information he may be possessing will do no injury to our army." Sent to Point Lookout, Maryland, he was transferred to Aikens Landing, Virginia, on March 15, 1865, for exchange. Russell died in Anderson, South Carolina, in 1924.

SCOTT, HUGH H. | Private, Company I, Second South Carolina Cavalry
Born in 1843 in Edgefield County, South Carolina, Scott enlisted on September 4, 1861. Detached as a scout on December 1, 1863, subsequent entries in his records and other accounts reflect this status remained

unchanged through the end of the war. Accounts suggest he was probably used as an occasional Scout as early as January 1863. Active postwar as a farmer, merchant and prolific writer of his wartime experiences, Scott went to Washington, D.C., and served as messenger for Senator Matthew C. Butler. He died in 1919.

SHADBURNE, GEORGE D. | Sergeant, Company A, Jeff Davis Legion
Born in 1842 in Brenham, Texas, Shadburne was the son of a hotel keeper from Kentucky and enlisted December 19, 1861. He was appointed fourth corporal on October 15, 1862, first corporal on April 15, 1863, and fifth sergeant on August 19, 1863. Shadburne was detached to serve as second commander of Hampton's Scouts on December 24, 1863. He signed an army requisition for two days' forage in Richmond on August 14, 1864, for "Eight private horses in the service of Genl Hampton's Scouts" with "G.D. Shadburne, Comdg Hampton's Scouts." This is the only known wartime document formally confirming the existence of Hampton's Scouts and Shadburne's status as their commander. Twice wounded, twice captured and twice escaped, his second escape was in March 1865 when he and Scout Jim Sloan slipped their shackles on a prison barge in the James River near City Point, Virginia. An attorney in San Francisco after the war, Shadburne wrote prolifically about his wartime experiences, named a son Wade Hampton and died in Alameda County, California, in 1921.

SHIRER, J. MARION | Color Sergeant, Company I, Second South Carolina Cavalry
Born in 1835 in Rembert, South Carolina, Shirer enlisted on June 6, 1861 in Columbia, South Carolina. The muster roll for November–December 1863 shows that he was absent on wounded furlough in South Carolina from December 10, 1863. He was detached as regimental color bearer and promoted to color sergeant on June 1, 1864. There are no records of his service as a Scout, but several accounts from other Scouts confirm his role. He is named as a member of the original platoon but likely rode as an occasional Scout. Shirer was cited by J.E.B. Stuart in a report for exceptional courage in the Mine Run Campaign with "Private J. Marion Shirer… was severely wounded while behaving with great gallantry." Also cited for heroism in *Butler and His Cavalry*, page 88. A physician after the war, he died in St. Stephens, South Carolina, in 1900.

SHIVER, ROBERT C. | Second Lieutenant, Company A, Second South Carolina Cavalry
Shiver was born about 1838 in Richland County, South Carolina, the son of a railroad agent and postmaster, and worked as a clerk prior to the war. He enlisted as a private on June 26, 1861, and was later brevetted to second lieutenant. Very little is found within his records, but a muster roll for January–February 1864 reports him as "absent on detached service near Yorktown from January 1864." Shiver was wounded in the right leg and captured on March 18, 1865, near Whitehall, North Carolina. Various sources describe him as "an early scout" and confirm that he rode occasionally with Hampton's Scouts, despite his rank. A dry goods merchant after the war, he died in Richland County in 1874.

SHOOLBRED, J.S. | Private, Company B, Second South Carolina Cavalry
Born about 1841 in Dorchester County, South Carolina, Shoolbred enlisted on June 19, 1861, at Grahamsville, South Carolina. Several references confirm he was in Hampton's Scouts from the earliest days until the war's end. He returned to Virginia with Hampton on April 20, 1864. Captured on March 30, 1863, Shoolbred spent a short while in Old Capitol Prison before being paroled. A farmer after the war, he died in Columbia, South Carolina, in 1872.

SLOAN, JAMES M. | Private, Company F, First North Carolina Cavalry
Sloan was born about 1843 in Cabarrus County, North Carolina, the son of a farmer. He enlisted on June 15, 1861, and various company muster rolls and accounts attest to continuous service as a Scout from early 1863 until April 1865. Sloan was captured at Catlett's Station, Virginia, on June 9, 1863, and exchanged at City Point on June 30, 1863. Later he was captured at Orleans, Virginia, on August 15, 1863, and sent to Point Lookout, Maryland, but he escaped on September 4, 1863. Sloan is credited with saving Shadburne's life in November 1864 and was captured with him in March 1865 but escaped from a prison barge on the James River, despite being shackled. A farmer and ferryman after the war, he died in Gaston County, North Carolina, in 1918.

SPARKS, JOHN CALHOUN | Color Sergeant, Company K, Second South Carolina Cavalry
Born about 1842 in Darlington County, South Carolina, Sparks enlisted on June 1, 1861, in Greenville, South Carolina, and was appointed regimental

color bearer on July 1, 1862. Records place him in a Richmond hospital from March 13 to 25, 1863, and he was killed while scouting (probably December 16, 1863) near Catlett's Station, Virginia. His body was later recovered by his brother and returned to South Carolina.

STARK, THOMAS LAMAR | Private, Company I, Second South Carolina Cavalry
Stark was born about 1844 in Jacksonville, Florida, the son of a planter. He enlisted on June 14, 1861, and was captured near Fredericksburg on May 3, 1863, and sent to Old Capitol Prison in Washington, D.C., on May 4. Muster rolls for May–June and July–August 1863 show he was absent on detached service. E.P. Henderson called him "the Brave Lamar Stark" in *Autobiography of Arab*. Stark was seriously wounded in 1864 action near Charleston. He was a postwar farmer and died in Columbia, South Carolina, in 1883.

TANNER, DANIEL F. | Private, Company I, Cobb's Legion
Tanner, brother of George C., was born about 1834 in North Carolina but living in Augusta, Georgia, as an artist prior to 1860. He enlisted on March 4, 1862, in Augusta, and was listed "Absent, Detailed as Scout by Gen'l Hampton August 25, 1864." However, accounts show him probably as an occasional Scout as early as January 1864. He resumed his art career after the war and died sometime after 1880.

TANNER, GEORGE C. | Private, Company I, Cobb's Legion
Tanner, Daniel's brother, was born about 1845 in North Carolina but living in Augusta, Georgia, and studying photography by 1860. He served with the First Georgia Infantry from March 18, 1861, to March 18, 1862, and was appointed the musician of Company I, Cobb's Legion, on April 1, 1862. Tanner was captured at Gettysburg on July 5, 1863, and wounded in action at the Wilderness on May 5, 1864. The occasional Scout died in 1924 at the Soldier's Home in Marietta, Georgia.

THISTLE, THOMAS T. | Private, Company A, Jeff Davis Legion
Thistle was born in Natchez, Mississippi, in 1839, the son of a planter. A medical student prior to the war, he enlisted on May 18, 1861, in Natchez. Records show him detached as a scout dating from December 24, 1863, and captured in November 1864. He had a medical career after the war and died in Louisiana in 1880.

THORNWELL, GILLESPIE | Private, Company H, Second South Carolina Cavalry
Thornwell was born in Columbia, South Carolina, in 1844, son of the most influential Presbyterian minister in the state. He enlisted on July 17, 1861, and was wounded and captured at Warrenton Junction, Virginia, on May 2, 1863, during a raid led by John Mosby. His wound was described as a gunshot wound to the abdomen, and he died on May 4, 1863, at the First Division General Hospital, "Mansion House," in Alexandria, Virginia. The last entry in his service record says his "body [was] taken away by his friends." Various accounts confirm his status as a Scout. Thornwell's body was retrieved and reburied at Columbia, South Carolina.

TORRY, RICHARD S. | Private, Company D, Jeff Davis Legion
Born about 1842, Torry enlisted on August 10, 1861, in Montgomery, Alabama. A muster roll covering May 1 through August 31, 1864, lists him "on detached service as Scout." Before the war, he was a farmer.

TURNER, W.H. | Private, Company B, Sixth South Carolina Cavalry
Enlisted on October 1, 1862, and detached as a scout on August 20, 1864, Turner was captured on November 28, 1864, on Jerusalem Plank Road and sent to Point Lookout on December 3, 1864. He was paroled and exchanged on February 18, 1865.

TWIGGS, JOSEPH A. | Private, Company K, First South Carolina Cavalry
Twiggs was born in Richmond County, Georgia, in 1843, the son of a planter. He enlisted on August 27, 1861, and the muster roll for November–December 1862 show him as "absent on scout," making him one of the earliest known of Hampton's Scouts. The September–October 1863 roll includes the same notation. Twice received furlough in 1863 to obtain a new horse, after the war, Twiggs was chief of police in Augusta, Georgia. He died in 1890.

WALLER, ARCHIBALD R. | Private, Company F, Jeff Davis Legion
Waller enlisted on April 1, 1862. His service record is sparse but confirms he was "absent on duty behind the enemy lines since January 7, 1864" at least into May 1864.

Waterbury, William M. | Sergeant, Company D, Third North Carolina Cavalry

Waterbury enlisted on May 17, 1862, and his service record is unique in that he was detailed to a wide variety of special assignments. From June 30, 1862, until September 20, 1864, when he was detailed as a scout, he served in a variety of special services. He was a courier; sergeant in charge of couriers; a telegraph operator in Petersburg, Virginia; and again in Fayetteville, North Carolina. Captured on November 19, 1864, below Petersburg with another Scout identified only as Morgan (probably a fictitious name), both escaped from the City Point stockade on December 14, 1864, causing much consternation among Union commanders. He was captured again, near Petersburg, on January 1, 1865. Taken at a local residence in a wounded condition (chest wound), Waterbury was placed under heavy guard and not moved until an army surgeon examined him and pronounced him capable of being returned to City Point. The Union correspondence within his record is amazing. An entry dated January 14, 1865, discharging him from the City Point hospital in preparation for his transfer to Point Lookout states, "This is the famous Rebel Scout who escaped and was wounded and recaptured." He was released from Point Lookout on June 19, 1865. Waterbury was said to have been a businessman in Baltimore after the war.

Willingham, John C. | Private, Company K, Second South Carolina Cavalry

Willingham enlisted on June 6, 1861, in Greenville, South Carolina. Company muster rolls for May–June and July–August 1863 mention that he was absent scouting. The September–October roll reads, "Absent, gone home on horse furlough" while the November–December roll states, "Absent on detached service." Also, there is a memorandum dated January 6, 1864, certifying that "he was detailed to scout in Fauquier County, VA & vicinity on 27 August 1863 & remained on this detail until October 22, 1863."

Notes

Introduction

1. Every effort has been made to accurately present events in sequential order. A few, however, are placed in a time frame based on reasoned judgement following intensive review of reference material lacking date of occurrence.

Chapter 2

2. *War of the Rebellion*, series 1, vol. 19, pt. 2, 709. Hereafter, this publication will be cited as *OR* and, unless otherwise noted, taken from series 1. Lee's use of "recruiting" reflects the 1860s military term meaning a complete stand-down for rebuilding and recovery. He accurately foresaw a lengthy stand-down as the only remedy allowing the horses of the cavalry to recover from their ailments.
3. Ibid., 709–10.
4. Henderson, *Autobiography of Arab*, 61–62. Full text available online at https://archive.org/details/autobiographyofa00hend.
5. Ibid., 62.
6. Ibid., 53–54. Henderson, writing almost forty years after the event, incorrectly referred to this battle as "Barber's Crossroads"; Latrelle E. Mickler, "William A. Mickler, Confederate Scout," *United Daughters of the Confederacy Magazine* 51, no.1 (January 1988): 79.

7. Henderson, *Autobiography of Arab*, 62.

8. Brooks, *Butler and His Cavalry*, 67.

9. Henderson, *Autobiography of Arab*, 63–64.

10. Ibid.; Brooks, *Butler and His Cavalry*, 162; *OR* 21:749–51, vol. 51, pt. 1, 971; "A Spirited Dash into the Enemy's Line," *Daily Courier* (Charleston, SC), January 22, 1863.

11. *OR* 21:749–51.

12. "Distinguished Service," *Daily Courier*, February 26, 1863. Butler's General Order and the ensuing letters were published in their entirety. A full account of the action involved was initially published in the *Richmond Examiner* and re-printed in the *Daily Courier* on January 22, 1863.

13. *OR* 21:750.

14. Henderson, in *Autobiography of Arab*, mentions the use of occasional scouts who, if needed and available, could be dispatched to Mickler. Henderson identifies himself as such in the early days but later was fully detached. Shirer and Butler also served in this capacity.

15. Henderson, *Autobiography of Arab*, 77.

Chapter 3

16. Brooks, *Butler and His Cavalry*, 136

17. *OR*, vol. 25, pt.1, 9.

18. "Sergeant Mickler's Last Scout," *Daily Courier*, March 20, 1863.

19. Ibid.; Henderson, *Autobiography of Arab*, 64.

20. Henderson, *Autobiography of Arab*, 65.

21. Ibid., 65–67.

22. Ibid., 69–70

23. Ibid., 67–73; On March 20, 1863, the *Daily Courier* detailed this action with an article titled "Sergeant Mickler's Last Scout."

24. *OR*, vol. 25, pt.1, 18–19, vol. 25, pt. 2, 649.

25. *Richmond Daily Dispatch*, February 18, 1863.

26. Henderson, *Autobiography of Arab*, 70–73; "Sergeant Mickler's Last Scout," *Daily Courier*, March 20, 1863.

27. Henderson, *Autobiography of Arab*, 71–73.

28. Brooks, *Butler and His Cavalry*, 101–2

Chapter 4

29. Henderson, *Autobiography of Arab*, 85.

30. Brooks, *Butler and His Cavalry*, 140.

31. Ibid.; Henderson, *Autobiography of Arab*, 96–99.

32. Brooks, *Butler and His Cavalry*, 139.

33. Henderson, *Autobiography of Arab*, 74–75.

34. Ibid., 76.

35. National Archives, Compiled Service Records of Confederate Soldiers Who Served in Organizations from the State of South Carolina, M267A, Roll 11 (Washington, D.C.) Microfilm.

36. Henderson, *Autobiography of Arab*, 80.

37. *OR*, vol. 25, pt. 2, 691.

38. Ibid., 700.

39. Ibid.

40. Ibid., 860.

41. Mosby, *Mosby's War Reminiscences*, 130.

42. Williamson, *Mosby's Rangers*, 56.

43. Henderson, *Autobiography of Arab*, 85–90, 99–100; Mosby, *Mosby's War Reminiscences*, 130–35; Williamson, *Mosby's Rangers*, 58; Brooks, *Butler and His Cavalry*, 233–34; Mosby's report to Stuart is found in *OR*, vol. 25, pt. 2, 861.

44. National Archives, M267A, Roll 14.

45. Hampton Family Papers, South Caroliniana Library, University of South Carolina, Columbia, South Carolina.

46. Henderson, *Autobiography of Arab*, 89, 106.

47. National Archives, *Compiled Service Records of Confederate Soldiers Who Served in Organizations from the State of Mississippi*, M269A, Roll 66; National Archives, M267A, Roll 11.

48. Henderson, *Autobiography of Arab*, 80–82, 115.

49. Ibid., 108–12.

50. Ibid., 113.

51. Ibid., 115.

52. Ibid., 114–16. Family records confirm the retrieval of Butler's remains.

53. Herndon, *Centennial History of Arkansas*, 1022–25.

Chapter 5

54. National Archives, M267A, Rolls 1, 13.

55. *OR*, vol. 27, pt. 1, 1057.

56. *OR*, vol. 29, pt. 1, 91–92; "Our Army Correspondence," *Richmond Daily Dispatch*, September 9, 1863.

57. *OR*, vol. 29, pt. 1, 102–3; Brooks, *Butler and His Cavalry*, 147; "Our Army Correspondence," *Richmond Daily Dispatch*, September 9–10, 1863.

58. *OR*, vol. 29, pt. 1, 102–3.

59. Ibid.

60. "Our Army Correspondence," *Richmond Daily Dispatch*, September 9–10, 1863.

61. Brooks, *Butler and His Cavalry*, 147.

62. Ibid., 162.

63. Ibid., 100–101. Hanley returned from his unauthorized absence several months later but was removed from the scouts' roster and suffered severe repercussions. See Annotated Roster for details.

64. *OR*, vol. 29, pt. 1, 496–97; Brooks, *Butler and His Cavalry*, 90–91.

65. Brooks, *Butler and His Cavalry*, 91.

66. Ibid.

67. Ibid.; Brooks, *Butler and His Cavalry*, 90–91.

68. National Archives, *Compiled Service Records of Confederate Soldiers Who Served in Organizations from the State of Georgia*, M266C, Rolls 0581, 0586; National Archives, M267A, Roll 6.

69. National Archives, M267A, Roll 12; The *Daily Courier*'s February 26, 1863 issue carried a letter from R.E. Lee to J.E.B. Stuart in which he states Sergeant Mickler, Sergeant Calhoun Sparks and Private Jack Shoolbred were all being recommended for promotion for "Gallantry and skill"; CSA War Department, *List of Appointments Made from the Ranks, from the Exhibition of Distinguished Valor and Skill in the Field* (Richmond, VA January 1864), https://archive.org/details/list of appointment.

Chapter 6

70. *OR*, vol. 29, pt. 1, 900.

71. Henderson, *Autobiography of Arab*, 82–83; National Archives, M267A, Rolls 12, 13.

72. National Archives, M269A, Roll 66; M267A, Roll 11.

73. National Archives, M269A, Rolls 70, 71.

74. Henderson, *Autobiography of Arab*, 133–34.

75. Ibid., 134–37.

76. Ibid.

77. Ibid., 137.

78. Ibid., 130.

79. National Archives. M269A, Rolls 66, 70. The Jeff Davis Legion, a Mississippi command, was unique in that it carried entire companies from Alabama and Georgia on its roster.

80. National Archives, M267A, Roll 11; Brooks, *Butler and His Cavalry*, 126.

81. National Archives, M267A, Roll 11.

Chapter 7

82. National Archives, M269A, Rolls 68, 69.

83. "After Separated 51 years, Old Veterans Hug and Weep: Russell Tells of Capt. Hogan's Assault on Yankee Camp during Civil War," Atkins (AK) *Chronicle*, May 26, 1916. Russell claimed the attack was on a brigade camp and at least five hundred Federals had surrendered before fighting was renewed. These claims are probably exaggerated.

84. Ibid.

85. Brooks, *Butler and His Cavalry*, 96–99; *OR* 33:154.

86. Brooks, *Butler and His Cavalry*, 98–99. Arrington's Crossroads was later renamed David's Crossroads and eventually became part of the U.S. Marine base at Quantico.

87. Ibid., 102.

88. *OR* 33:201.

89. Brooks, *Butler and His Cavalry*, 102–3.

90. *OR* 33:201–2.

91. Brooks, *Butler and His Cavalry*, 123–25.

92. Ibid., 123–28; National Archives, M266C, Roll 0581; M269A, Roll 66; M267A, Roll 6.

93. National Archives, M269A, Roll 68, 69; Hopkins, *Little Jeff*, 188.

94. National Archives, M269A, Rolls 68, 69.

95. Henderson, *Autobiography of Arab*, 142.

96. Ibid.

Chapter 8

97. *OR*, 33:1259–60.

98. National Archives, M267A, Rolls 5, 6, 11, 12, 13.

99. Ibid., Rolls 5, 12.

100. Brooks, *Butler and His Cavalry*, 417–18.

101. Ibid., 129, 489–91.

102. Ibid., 308.

103. Bessie Bagby, "Thrilling Escape of Federal Prisoners," *Confederate Veteran* 16 (1908): 392; Brooks, *Butler and His Cavalry*, 109–10.

104. Bagby, "Thrilling Escape of Federal Prisoners," 392.

105. Ibid.

106. Ibid.; Brooks, *Butler and His Cavalry*, 109.

107. *OR* 33:857.

108. "From Northern Virginia," *Richmond Daily Dispatch*, May 4, 1864.

109. Joseph Frederick Waring Papers, Southern Historical Collection, UNC, Chapel Hill, North Carolina.

110. "From Northern Virginia," *Richmond Daily Dispatch*, May 6, 1864.

111. "Accounts of the Battle," *Richmond Daily Dispatch*, May 9, 1864.

112. "Operations in Northern Virginia," *Richmond Daily Dispatch*, May 16, 1864.

113. Waring Papers.

114. Ibid.; Hopkins, *Little Jeff*, 198.

115. Lee, *Recollections and Letters*, 124–25.

116. Brooks, *Butler and His Cavalry*, 141–42.

Chapter 9

117. Waring Papers.

118. Brooks, *Butler and His Cavalry*, 106–7.

119. Ibid., 268–69. Hampton's report concerning these operations can also be found in *OR* 36:1095–97.

120. Brooks, *Butler and His Cavalry*, 107.

121. Wells, *Hampton and His Cavalry*, 243–44; Hopkins, *Little Jeff*, 219.

122. Brooks, *Butler and His Cavalry*, 280–82; *Confederate Veteran* 22, 409; "Cavalry Scouts—Shadbourne," *Land We Love* 3 (August 1867): 348–51.

123. Brooks, *Butler and His Cavalry*, 281.

124. Ibid. No records are found attesting to Shadburne being promoted to captain. It is very likely he was offered the promotion under the Valor

and Skill Act of 1862 but declined it, for it would have taken him from scouting.

125. *OR*, vol. 40, pt. 1, 807–10; Hopkins, *Little Jeff*, 215.

Chapter 10

126. John S. Elliott, "Annals of the War," (Philadelphia) *Weekly Times*, May 3, 1884.
127. Waring Papers.
128. *OR*, vol. 40, pt. 3, 325.
129. Ibid.
130. Waring Papers.
131. Ibid.
132. Ibid. The Jeff Davis legion carried several men with the Williams surname, none of whom are mentioned in other sources as scouts. It is impossible to identify Ashby's companion other than to say he might have been an occasional scout not mentioned elsewhere.
133. Ibid. Torbert's division was being sent to Sheridan in the Shenandoah Valley.
134. *OR*, vol. 42, pt. 2, 164–65.
135. Ibid., 583.
136. Elliott, "Annals of the War."
137. Ibid.
138. Ibid.
139. Ibid. Analysis of Elliott's account indicates the Union force was squadron or battalion sized.
140. Ibid.
141. National Archives, M269A, Roll 70.
142. National Archives, M267A, Roll 44; M266C, Roll 0589.

Chapter 11

143. Elliott, "Annals of the War."
144. Ibid.; Brooks, *Butler and His Cavalry*, 111.
145. *OR*, vol. 42, pt. 2, 1235–36.
146. Ibid.,1242.
147. *Confederate Veteran* 22, no. 4 (April 1914): 166.

148. Brooks, *Butler and His Cavalry*, 111–12; Elliott, "Annals of the War"; Wells, *Hampton and His Cavalry*, 302–3.

149. *OR*, vol. 42, pt. 1, 944–47.

150. Brooks, *Butler and His Cavalry*, 103.

151. Ibid., 104.

152. *OR*, vol. 42, pt. 2, 681.

153. Ibid., 716.

154. Ibid., 716, 756, 810, 814, 933, vol. 42, pt. 1, 204.

Chapter 12

155. National Archives, M267A, Rolls 4, 27, 42; M269A, Roll 70; M270A, Roll 0025.

156. Brooks, *Butler and His Cavalry*, 111.

157. *OR*, vol. 42, pt. 3, 177.

158. Brooks, *Butler and His Cavalry*, 509–12. Writing in 1907, Russell misidentifies Kennedy as F.M. McClure.

159. National Archives, M267A, Rolls 6, 12.

160. Waring Papers.

161. Ibid.

162. "Hampton's Splendid Scout, Jim Sloan," *The* (Columbia, SC) *State*, May 12, 1902, 6.

163. Ibid.

164. Ibid.

165. National Archives, M267A, Rolls 5, 44; M270A, Roll 0025; M269A, Roll 71.

166. Waring Papers.

167. "The War News," *Richmond Daily Dispatch*, November 15, 1864; (Raleigh, NC) *Weekly Standard*, November 16, 1864.

168. Waring Papers.

169. Brooks, *Butler and His Cavalry*, 105.

170. Ibid.

171. Ibid., 109–10; *Confederate Veteran* 16 (1908): 391–92.

172. Brooks, *Butler and His Cavalry*, 106.

173. Ibid.

174. Ibid.

Chapter 13

175. Hopkins, *Little Jeff*, 247.
176. Brooks, *Butler and His Cavalry*, 411.
177. Ibid.
178. *OR*, vol. 42, pt.1, 98, vol. 42, pt. 3, 866; Wells, *Hampton and His Cavalry*, 383.
179. Trudeau, *Last Citadel*, 277.
180. Ibid., 272.
181. Brooks, *Butler and His Cavalry*, 412.
182. Ibid.
183. Ibid.; Hopkins, *Little Jeff*, 249; *Confederate Veteran* 22 (1914): 408.
184. Trudeau, *Last Citadel*, 280, 282–83.
185. *OR*, vol. 42, pt. 1, 356–57.
186. Brooks, *Butler and His Cavalry*, 11, 387; Trudeau, *Last Citadel*, 280. Perhaps the best account of this raid is that of Chris Calkins found in "Apple Jack Raid," *Blue & Gray* 22, no. 3 (Summer 2005): 18–25.
187. Longacre, *Gentleman and Soldier*, 221.

Chapter 14

188. Hopkins, *Little Jeff*, 256.
189. Brooks, *Butler and His Cavalry*, 390. Shadburne's list came from memory many years after the war and has a couple of errors. He also named Daniel Latham and Creel (believed to have been Solomon Legare), who were both in Union prisoner-of-war camps.
190. "Affairs Below Petersburg," *Richmond Daily Dispatch*, February 13, 1865; Brooks, *Butler and His Cavalry*, 389–90; *Confederate Veteran* 12 (1904): 121–22.
191. Brooks, *Butler and His Cavalry*, 390–92.
192. "Affairs Below Petersburg."
193. Ibid., February 25, 1865.
194. *OR*, vol. 46, pt.1, 543.
195. Ibid.
196. Ibid., 542–44; Brooks, *Butler and His Cavalry*,104–5, 393–402.

Chapter 15

197. Brooks, *Butler and His Cavalry*, 403–4. Sanders was a civilian guide.
198. Ibid., 404–7.
199. Ibid., 408.
200. Ibid., 505.
201. Ibid.
202. Ibid., 506.
203. Ibid., 422.
204. Ibid.
205. Ibid., 506, 491.
206. Ibid., 112. Slightly different versions of this morning's events exist in a variety of books and magazines. Some say that Scott reported that not over fifteen Yankees were in town.
207. Ibid., 408. Scout John Colvin gave a written detailed account in which he stated he was a member of the party accompanying Hampton in the fighting. However, he is not one of those named in Hampton's letter of March 19 outlining the engagement.
208. Ibid., 112–13.
209. Andrew, *Wade Hampton*, 178–79; Wells, *Hampton and His Cavalry*, 173–74; Brooks, *Butler and His Cavalry*, 113.
210. Hampton is credited by historians with killing at least thirteen Federal soldiers in close combat, as a general, with his revolver or his sword. Some raise that figure to as many as eighteen.
211. Brooks, *Butler and His Cavalry*, 463–64.
212. *OR*, vol. 47, pt. 2, 1113.
213. Andrew, *Wade Hampton*, 289–90; Wittenberg, *Battle of Monroe's Crossroads*, 209.
214. Ibid.
215. National archives, M267A, Rolls 5, 42; Brooks, *Butler and His Cavalry*, 513.

Epilogue

216. Brooks, *Butler and His Cavalry*, 513, 418.
217. Ibid., 147.
218. Ibid., 287.

Bibliography

Books and Articles

Andrew, Rod, Jr. *Wade Hampton, Confederate Warrior to Southern Redeemer.* Chapel Hill: University of North Carolina Press, 2008.

Brooks, U.R. *Butler and His Cavalry in the War of Secession, 1861–1865.* Columbia, SC: State Company, 1909.

Calkins, Chris, "The Apple Jack Raid, 'For This Barbarism There Was No Real Excuse.'" *Blue & Gray* 22, no. 3 (Summer 2005).

"Cavalry Scouts—Shadburne." *Land We Love* 3 (August 1867).

Confederate Veteran Magazine. 40 vols., Nashville, TN: n.p.; 1892–1932.

Henderson, E. Prioleau. *Autobiography of Arab.* Columbia, SC: R.L. Bryan Company, 1901.

Herndon, Dallas. *Centennial History of Arkansas.* Chicago: Southern Historical Press, 1922.

Hopkins, Donald A. *The Little Jeff: The Jeff Davis Legion, Cavalry, Army of Northern Virginia.* Shippensburg, PA: White Mane Books, 1999.

Lee, Captain Robert E. *Recollections and Letters of Robert E. Lee.* Old Saybrook, CT: Konecky & Konecky, 1924.

Longacre, Edward G. *Gentleman and Soldier: The Extraordinary Life of General Wade Hampton.* Nashville, TN: Rutledge Hill Press, 2003.

Mickler, Latrelle E. "William A. Mickler, Confederate Scout." *United Daughters of the Confederacy Magazine* 51, no. 1 (January 1988).

Mosby, John S. *Mosby's War Reminiscences, Stuart's Cavalry Campaign.* New York: Dodd, Mead and Company, 1898.

Trudeau, Noah Andre. *The Last Citadel: Petersburg, Virginia, June 1864–April 1865.* Baton Rouge: Louisiana State University Press, 1991.

Wells, Edward L. *Hampton and His Cavalry in '64.* Richmond, VA: Johnson, 1899.

Williamson, James J. *Mosby's Rangers, a Record of the Forty-Third Battalion Virginia Cavalry from Its Organization to the Surrender.* New York: Ralph B. Kenton, 1896.

Wittenberg, Eric J. *Battle of Monroe's Crossroads and the Civil War's Final Campaign.* New York: Savas Beatie, 2006.

Archival Depositories

CSA War Department. "List of Appointments Made from the Ranks, from the Exhibition of Distinguished Valor and Skill in the Field and Who Have Taken the Positions to which They Have Been Respectfully Appointed." (Richmond, January 1864). https.//archive.org/details/list of appointmen00conf.

Hampton Family Papers, South Caroliniana Library, University of South Carolina, Columbia.

National Archives. *Compiled Service Records of Confederate Soldiers Who Served in Organizations from the State of Georgia, M266C,* Rolls *581, 586, 589; Compiled Service Records of Confederate Soldiers Who Served in Organizations from the State of North Carolina, M270A,* Rolls 5, 7-9, 25; *Compiled Service Records of Confederate Soldiers Who Served in Organizations from the State of Mississippi, M269A,* Rolls 66-71; *Compiled Services of Confederate Soldiers Who Served in Organizations from the State of South Carolina, M267A,* Rolls 1, 5–7, 10–14, 24, 27, 33, 42, 44.

Southern Historical Collection, University of North Carolina. Special Collection. *Joseph Frederick Waring Papers, Collection M-1664.* Chapel Hill, North Carolina.

The War of the Rebellion: A Compilation of the Official Records of the Union and Confederate Armies. 128 volumes. Washington, D.C.: Government Printing Office, 1880–1901.

Newspapers

(Atkins, AK) *Chronicle*, 1916.
(Charleston, SC) *Daily Courier*, 1863–1864.
The (Columbia, SC) *State*, 1902.
(Philadelphia) *Free Press*, 1884
(Raleigh, NC) *Weekly Standard*, 1864
(Richmond, VA) *Daily Dispatch*, 1863–1865.

INDEX

A

Adams, Joel R. 85, 108
Ashby, Walter S. 75, 102, 108, 133

B

Barnwell, Woodward 34, 37, 38,
  108
Beck, Josiah 24, 37, 54, 109
Black, Franklin H. "Gus" 40, 109
Bolick, William A. 43, 47, 49, 54,
  58, 59, 109
Bradley, John A. 38, 54, 109
Brent, James H. 50, 54, 60, 110
Butler, Matthew C. 12, 61, 64, 72,
  76, 89, 92, 94, 99, 100
Butler, Thomas L. 24, 31, 41, 110

C

Carroll, S.L. 55, 60, 61, 110
Chapman, John L. 55, 63, 86, 106,
  110
Cloud, Daniel 71
Cloyd, T. Shelby 53, 110
Colvin, John C. 44, 85, 98, 99, 111,
  136
Crafton, George M. 24, 111
Curtis, Isaac 49, 92

D

Dulin, James R. 24, 38, 49, 64, 98,
  99, 100, 111

E

Eison, N.B. 85, 102, 111
Elliott, John S. 55, 63, 73, 75, 78,
  81, 86, 87, 89, 112, 133, 134

F

Fowles, John Newton 38, 40, 53, 100, 112

G

Guffin, James T. 64, 69, 98, 112
Guffin, Lemuel L. 64, 106, 113
Guffin, L. Pemberton 64, 112

H

Hampton, Wade 11, 13, 20, 21, 24, 37, 38, 40, 42, 51, 52, 58, 59, 61, 63, 65, 69, 70, 72, 76, 78, 81, 83, 87, 91, 94, 98, 100, 102, 105
Hanley, George J. 24, 32, 48, 113
Harris, J.S. 63, 72, 81, 86, 87, 108, 113
Harrison, J.J. 55, 61, 113
Haskell, William E. 38, 113
Henagan, A. Bernard 24, 54, 55, 114
Henderson, E.P. 12, 13, 21, 24, 33, 36, 37, 40, 52, 54, 61, 107, 114
Hodges, William H. 55, 63, 114
Hogan, J. Dickerson 24, 32, 40, 41, 45, 47, 48, 54, 56, 57, 58, 64, 71, 74, 76, 82, 83, 84, 85, 98, 99, 114, 131
Hord, William H. 57, 63, 115
Hutchinson, Phillip H. 85, 87, 115

J

Johnson, R. Cecil 24, 31, 41, 115

K

Kennedy, W. Adolphus 64, 70, 86, 115, 120, 134
King, T. Bernard 64, 69, 106, 115
Knapp, A. Champion 55, 61, 116

L

Latham, Daniel F. 55, 61, 116
Lee, Fitzhugh 14, 20, 37
Lee, Robert E. 11, 13, 15, 18, 32, 38, 45, 49, 66, 68, 76, 81, 87, 91, 105
Legare, Solomon E. 85, 86, 87, 103, 105, 116, 119
Lide, Leighton W. 116
Logan, Roswell F. 38, 117

M

McCalla, James D. 64, 82, 83, 106, 117
McClure, F.M. 117, 134
McCoy, A.J. 57, 61, 117
McIlwayne, John H. 94, 117
Merchant, Rufus B. 50, 54, 63, 81, 118
Mickler, Huger 24, 28, 40, 118
Mickler, William A. 21, 24, 26, 29, 32, 33, 36, 37, 40, 42, 50, 52, 106, 118

Miller, Simeon E. 24, 39, 118
Miller, W. Wallace 24, 31, 48, 64, 69, 71, 72, 87, 103, 105, 119
Morrow, William B. 64, 119

N

Niblet, Jim 83, 119

P

Parks, William P. 24, 63, 119
Pierce, John H. 50, 54, 60, 120

R

Rife, William W. 72, 85, 87, 94, 120
Russell, W. Walker 50, 54, 57, 58, 64, 69, 82, 86, 115, 120, 131, 134

S

Scott, Hugh H. 34, 48, 54, 58, 59, 60, 64, 70, 71, 82, 83, 89, 90, 100, 101, 102, 120
Shadburne, George D. 11, 52, 54, 57, 61, 63, 66, 67, 69, 70, 72, 74, 75, 79, 81, 83, 85, 86, 89, 91, 93, 94, 96, 102, 106, 121
Shephard, Dick 22
Shirer, Marion J. 24, 121, 128
Shiver, Robert C. 33, 34, 122
Shoolbred, J.S. 24, 25, 37, 54, 64, 98, 122, 130

Sloan, James M. 24, 40, 49, 54, 63, 72, 86, 87, 94, 96, 97, 121, 122, 134
Sparks, J. Calhoun 24, 25, 34, 40, 52, 53, 122, 130
Stark, T. Lamar 39, 123
Stuart, J.E.B. 11, 12, 13, 14, 15, 16, 17, 18, 20, 24, 25, 28, 29, 30, 32, 35, 38, 39, 43, 45, 46, 47, 49, 52, 54, 55, 59, 62, 63, 66, 68, 69, 76, 79, 96, 105, 111, 129, 130

T

Tanner, Daniel F. 59, 60, 72, 80, 94, 123
Tanner, George C. 123
Thistle, Thomas T. 53, 63, 87, 90, 123
Thornwell, Gillespie 34, 38, 39, 40, 124
Torry, Richard S. 63, 124
Towles, Bob 22
Turner, W.H. "Bill" 80, 87, 124
Twiggs, Joseph A. 54, 124

W

Waller, Archibald 55, 63, 94, 124
Waring, J. Frederick 53, 67, 70, 75, 86, 87, 89, 132, 133, 134
Waterbury, William M. 85, 87, 125
Willingham, John C. 24, 54, 125

ABOUT THE AUTHOR

Michael Thomas is a life-long student of southern history with special emphasis on the War Between the States. He holds a BA in history from The Citadel and is a U.S. Navy veteran of Vietnam. He spent several years as a volunteer with the Chesterfield Historical Society of Virginia doing research and writing on Chesterfield County Confederate soldiers. He coached and umpired Little League Baseball for thirteen years and, later, spent several years as a WBTS reenactor. Now retired after thirty-one years in international trade, he is back in his home state of South Carolina. This is his first book.